The Disappearance of Amy Wroe Bechtel

Pete Dove

Published by Trellis Publishing, 2021.

While every precaution has been taken in the preparation of this book, the publisher assumes no responsibility for errors or omissions, or for damages resulting from the use of the information contained herein.

THE DISAPPEARANCE OF AMY WROE BECHTEL

First edition. July 13, 2021.

Copyright © 2021 Pete Dove.

ISBN: 979-8224458189

Written by Pete Dove.

THE DISAPPEARANCE OF AMY WROE BECHTEL

PETE DOVE

Running into Danger

Young love is infectious. The future is an open book, each page to be filled as the couple go along. Hope blossoms; everything is rosy.

Amy Wroe Bechtel and her husband Steve were an active, outdoor adventure type couple making the small town of Lander, Wyoming a perfect location for their second home together. They had only recently moved into their compact ex miner's cottage on Climbers Row when their paradise was punctured. Because, on July 24th, 1997, Amy disappeared.

She was an outstanding runner who had a personal best marathon time of just over three hours. Amy believed that, with hard training, she could qualify for the marathon trials for the US team which would head for Sydney in three years' time. Steve's sport was climbing, and he was becoming an expert in his field. The Shoshone National Forest, right on their new doorstep, provided opportunities for Steve to climb steep gorges and vertical cliffs, while offering challenging tracks for Amy to develop her own talents. A perfect combination for the adventurous couple.

Lander of 2019 is a very different place to the small town of 1997. Today it is a panacea for outdoor types. Sinks Canyon lies shortly outside the town's boundary and is home to a huge range of challenges of the kind climbers love. The National Outdoor Leadership School is situated nearby, and Lander is a Mecca to the growing road race and ultra-running community. But it is also rural Wyoming and cowhands share the stools propping up the well-known Lander bar with those still known as 'rock rats'. It is one such enthusiast that owns that popular local hostelry.

In fact, the Lander bar is one of the few connections between the town of 2019 and its younger self from 1997. Back then, the local population regarded the adventurous climbing community with some suspicion. They saw the influx of young men and women as an invasion of their territory by time wasters who were reluctant to work and contributed little to the life of their town. That perception has, fortunately, now largely changed.

Amy and Steve were among the first swathe of outdoor adventure junkies to reside there and managed to combine their love of the outdoors with both work and establishing their new home. Amy really was a promising runner and her chances of making the Olympic team were much more than a pipe dream. She ranked first in school history in the indoor 3000m with a time of 9.48 and second in the 5000m having achieved a time of 18.07 in 1995. Running was her passion and she committed herself to the kind of training routine which could deliver the dreams she longed to realise.

But she needed to earn a living as well. Along with her husband she worked part time at the Wild Iris store, a local shop servicing the climbing community. She was also a waitress at the Sweetwater Grill and taught weightlifting class to young people at the Wind River fitness centre. Now, with their new home on Lucky Lane, the future really did contain a rose-coloured hue, with or without similarly tinted glasses.

With such a busy schedule Amy needed to be a highly organised person; and she was. On the day she disappeared she had prepared a checklist of jobs to be completed before she could commit herself to a substantial training run. 'Get the work done and then have some fun' seemed to be her motto. Steve had a more leisurely day planned, even if it was a strenuous one. He was off climbing with a close friend. That friend would provide him with a very much needed alibi when police attention suddenly focused on him a few days after his wife's disappearance.

Amy's plan was to start the day by teaching a weightlifting class at the fitness centre. With a sensitivity to the environment typical of active outdoor types her next job was to carry a carload of waste to the local recycling centre and from there she would be headed to a photo store called Camera Connection. Her tight schedule saw her hoping to get to the store by around 2:30 PM. Photography was a keen hobby of

Amy's and she was planning to enter a local competition in the near future.

While at the photography store she had a friendly chat with the owner, Greg Wagner. Although there was little unusual about their conversation, Wagner did notice that Amy looked at her watch several times while they were talking. It was as though she had an appointment to keep. Her clock watching was something Greg barely registered at the time, but which seemed to take on added significance in the light of what was about to happen.

Because her conversation with Greg was the last time she was seen before her disappearance. Amy's next job was to drive to an area close to the Shoshone National Forest where she planned to sketch out a 10 kilometre run she was jointly organising with the local gym. The other job on her itinerary that day was to go for a run herself.

Meanwhile, back in Lander, Steve returned home at about 4:30 in the afternoon. Although Amy was not there, this did not cause any alarm as he knew she had a busy day planned. It was only as the hours began to pass with no sign of his wife that Steve began to get a little concerned. The time they ate dinner came and went and minor anxiety in Steve developed into more serious worries. By 10:30 pm, with darkness set in and still no sign of Amy, Steve decided it was time to take some action.

Yet even then he could see several possible explanations for the fact that his wife was not at home. Some more innocent than others. As a result, when he phoned the police to report her missing, it was almost as though he was embarrassed by the whole situation.

'Uh, yeah, hey, I've got a person missing here, I think, and I wondered if you had a spare around any place?' The nervously facetious tone of his enquiry was not the kind of panicked call that police were used to receiving when a person reported a problem. But Steve was an active young man used to dealing with climbing crises and to report his wife missing seemed incongruous to him. Later, the strange tone and language of the phone call would be used by some to suggest his guilt. However, with the benefit of more than twenty years of hindsight we can see that the slightly jokey, mildly uncomfortable tone he employed was not really a cause for concern. Unusual, yes; but not alarming.

The next day, July 25th, Amy's Toyota Tercel vehicle was found in the vicinity of Frye Lake, about half a mile from the banks of the local beauty spot. It appeared as though the car had been abandoned. There was no sign of Amy, and her wallet was missing. But otherwise, all seemed calm. It did not look as though she had left the car to go on her run, because her sunglasses and car keys were still on the passenger seat. Near them was the to do list which gave an insight into her day, scrawled on a scrappy piece of paper with each item checked as it was completed.

The only exception was her final task of the day, which simply said 'Run'. There was no indication of any kind of struggle in or near the vehicle and although some pools of water had formed by the rear tyres of the car, left by a storm which hit the area the previous day, there was no evidence of muddy tracks which might suggest the car had been driven off the narrow road.

One possibility which began to briefly raise its head was that the anxiety regarding the time that she had displayed in Camera Connection was connected to a secretive plan she had to meet with somebody. However, nothing beyond idle supposition supported that conclusion. Further, her 'to do' list made no reference to such a scheme. But then again, nothing about Amy's disappearance made any obvious sense.

Steve led the supportive local climbing community as they began their search for Amy. Two dozen of his friends, some on quad bikes and other ATVs, helped him in his increasingly desperate endeavour. Soon numbers swelled until more than a hundred volunteers were out looking for the twenty-four-year-old Olympic hopeful. Everything from dogs to dirt bikes were employed in their quest. While such community spirit is to be commended, the unintended effect of their zeal was to turn the area around where her car had been found into a zone which now provided no use whatsoever to the police. Their failure to seal off the crime scene, if indeed that is what it was, led to considerable criticism of the local Police Department in the coming years. To be fair, though, at the time her disappearance was not considered to be a crime; people were confident that she would be found, perhaps lost or even injured, somewhere in the dense woods. A hope that has never been made reality.

Sergeant John Zerga has worked on the investigation into Amy's disappearance for many years. He was assigned to it as a cold case in 2010 and has some explanation as to why the crime scene was allowed to be trampled on by well-meaning but unskilled volunteers.

'Here's the whole problem. Nowadays, everything is viewed as a homicide.' he said 'Back then it wasn't viewed that way; she was just a missing runner for three days. '

Numerous theories have grown up over the years as to what may have happened to Amy. The first of these still remains a possibility. However, the notion that she fell victim to mother nature struggles to survive under scrutiny. The theory goes that whilst out on her run either the environment or the varied wildlife which lives within it led to her downfall.

The idea begins to lose credibility when it is remembered that Amy left her keys and sunglasses in her car along but took her wallet with her. It is odd to leave your keys in your vehicle even in such a quiet and remote location as the Shoshine Forest. Equally strange is that if Amy felt it safe to leave her keys, she did not feel the same about her wallet. However, we know that both she and Steve were delighted about the community into which they had moved. Both were young and trusting and perhaps the idea that her car may be stolen simply did not register with her. We can only surmise.

The area is home to bears, snakes, coyotes and other animals which could, under certain circumstances, become a threat to a human. If a person disturbed or surprised them or threatened their young – a person such as a runner crashing through the undergrowth - they could be prompted to attack. The possibility that Amy was a victim of such an incident is unlikely. But not impossible.

Yet at no stage has evidence emerged to suggest that she was attacked by a wild animal. No blood or body parts or bones have ever been discovered. No torn clothing has been found hanging from a bush or trampled into the ground. But while this makes the idea of an animal attack highly unlikely, it is not unheard of for people to vanish without a trace of evidence being found. Then many years later for something to emerge which suggests they were indeed the victim of a wild animal.

As we have seen, the area is a climber's paradise and so it is also possible that Amy stumbled and fell from her path, meeting her death in some remote ravine or down some rarely visited cliff. However, given the time that has elapsed since her disappearance, and the popularity of the region, such a happening is unlikely because some evidence of her body would surely have been found. Unless, of course, having fallen, injured or killed herself her body was then dragged away by a predator.

Another possible explanation for Amy's disappearance is that she chose to run away. Perhaps, despite the apparently ordered routine of her day, she had arranged to meet with somebody and that explained the frequent glances at her watch in the camera store noted by Greg Wagner. It may be that completing such an overtly ordinary day was some part of a ruse to hide her intentions. Possibly she left her keys in the hope that people would assume she had become lost on a run but took her wallet because it contained cards that she needed.

Such a scenario seems unlikely, however. It would be an astonishingly elaborate smokescreen to create. In addition to this her friends and neighbours indicated that she seemed to be very happy with her life. Although (as we will see later) there is some evidence to suggest that what appeared on the surface to be a very happy marriage was not quite as idyllic as was presented to the world, there is nothing to suggest she wished to run away from it.

Similarly, if she had just chosen to start her life anew, to do so from some isolated running path in the middle of nowhere made her job considerably harder than it might have been. Again, absolutely nothing to suggest that she wished to begin her life afresh (or indeed end it) has ever been found and if she is still alive, she has avoided communicating with anybody from her past life for more than twenty years. Friends, family, parents. But for all of this, some people note that there were some indications that relations between the sporty couple were not all that they seemed on the surface.

Which brings us neatly and sadly to the two most widely expressed explanations for the disappearance of Amy. The first of these centres around husband Steve.

Amy and Steve had been married for just a year and a month when she disappeared. They had graduated together from the University of Wyoming, each holding a degree in exercise physiology from the Laramie institution. The couple's Climbers' Row cottage was owned by friends of theirs; Todd Skinner and Amy Whisler, who too were involved with the sport of climbing. In fact, Skinner was Steve's usual climbing partner, although was not with him on the day Amy disappeared. Skinner died in a fall in Yosemite in 2006 but in 1997 he was a rising start of the climbing community.

It was Todd and his partner who found Amy's Toyota the day after she disappeared. Of course, although their intentions were the best, by the time they had searched the car and even driven it back to Steve's home, as a source of evidence for the police it was seriously compromised.

Despite the support given to Steve in his search for Amy the community was suspicious. Bryan Di Salvatore was a writer for an outdoor sports magazine who covered the case. 'That town was freaked out. Scared and angry.' he said.

it was the lack of a body and any clear indication of how or why Amy had disappeared that first saw Steve brought under the unpleasant light of suspicion. For the first few days her disappearance had not even been considered a crime until it slowly dawned on the authorities that they could have a kidnapping, or even a murder on their hands. Then, pressure began to grow on them to identify a suspect.

But to a large extent the horse had bolted, its stable door left open by poor judgment from the law enforcement authorities. 'We didn't close off any route out of here. We didn't close off any vehicles. All we had was a bunch of people up here looking for a missing runner,' Sergeant Zerga, based in his small office in Fremont County Sheriff's Office in Lander, bemoans. 'We actually ruined it with the vehicle, because we allowed the Skinners to drive it home. The investigation was not good for at least the first three days; there was a lot of stuff that was lost.'

John Gookin PHD is a search and rescue expert who was a leading figure in the coordinated search for Amy. He too recognised the amateurish nature of the police work. The man best equipped to lead the investigation was away at the time Amy disappeared, and his replacement was not up to the job. Gookin said: 'He was off in the mountains on a horse packing trip so this guy who had just been promoted to detective from jailer was in charge of the search. The promoted jailer asked me "Well what do I do?"'

Then on August 5th an FBI agent accused Steve of being his wife's killer. Rick McCullough based his accusations on some entries found in both Steve's and Amy's journals. Up until that point Steve had been keen to help in any way he could. However, he sensed the way the investigation was moving and feared that he could be framed for his wife's disappearance. The police claimed they had hard evidence backing up their accusations; but they did not. They were lying, and the final branch of trust between investigators and mourning husband was broken. The only clue they had was a report from a local woman. She claimed to have seen a truck similar to the one driven by Steve in the vicinity of Amy's disappearance during the approximate time she went missing. But her evidence was purely circumstantial, and the woman did not claim to be able to make a firm identification of either the driver or the truck.

The other evidence upon which the police were basing their assumptions was equally lightweight. In Steve's journal they had come across some references to violence towards women and Amy in particular. Then in her diary there were some comments which could - and it is important to note the word 'could '– be interpreted to suggest that Steve had a controlling nature.

On this dubious evidence the police requested Steve take a polygraph test. However, he was very concerned about how any results may be interpreted and, on the advice of his lawyer, refused. Some members of the community, the police and the media took his refusal as evidence of guilt; but such an interpretation is little more than an unsubstantiated leap of faith.

Let us just place ourselves in Steve's position for a moment. His wife has gone missing and she is feared dead. His life has been turned upside down. When their future seemed so good and they had just moved into the ideal home in a location that both adored he was suddenly left on his own. Then as he desperately searched for any sign of his missing wife, his emotions alternating between hope and fear, he is accused of her murder. Out of the blue. The police claim they have hard evidence when he knows that none exists, and they ask that he takes a polygraph test. Who, knowing they are innocent, would not be suspicious were such a request be made to them?

Further, Steve had the perfect alibi which proved he could not have committed the crime. At the time his wife went missing he was halfway up a cliff face, climbing with his friend Sam Lightner in some mountains near Dubois, seventy miles away.

The only other evidence ever to appear to link Steve even remotely with the crime is a comment made by Amy's brother Nels. He tells of a time the two were visiting for dinner. Amy had some bruising and when Nel commented on this she laughed it off saying 'Steve can get a little rough sometimes.'

But Amy was a highly active sportswoman. Bruises were an everyday part of life for her; a consequence of her tough training regime. Her throwaway comment could be interpreted literally, but more likely it was just the sort of jokey comment many people make from time to time.

So realistically Steve cannot be considered a suspect in his wife's disappearance and almost certain death. In some ways, he has been able to move on from his tragedy, although it must still haunt him daily, and he did at least go on to remarry. As for Amy, she was declared legally dead in 2004.

So, it would seem as though Amy's disappearance would remain a mystery unlikely ever to be solved. But then another extremely plausible suspect appeared on the horizon. Dale Wayne Eaton is a convicted murderer and probably serial killer currently waiting to meet his own judgement day on death row. His brother and sister in law told police that Eaton had been camped out in the area around that in which Amy most probably disappeared during the time she vanished. Just six weeks later he attempted to kidnap a family whose car had broken down in the Burnt Gulch region. He went on to kill Lisa Marie Kimmell, and is suspected of being the man responsible for a number of women who died in what are known as the Great Basin Murders, which occurred between 1983 and 1996.

Eaton has consistently refused to discuss the possibility of his involvement in Amy's disappearance. That can be interpreted in two ways. It may be, as Steve believes, that Eaton's refusal to talk on the subject simply reflects his lack of involvement in it.

'As much as Eaton makes an attractive suspect, I don't think we're ever going to learn anything from him,' says Steve 'I think trying to point the finger at him just provides a convenient answer in a situation where there are no answers.' It seems clear that Steve believes his wife's probable murder will never be solved.

However, for others the coincidence of a murderer living rough in the very region where Amy disappeared is too much to be ignored. Did she pass him by the roadside and stop to speak? Amy was a kind and outgoing person. Stopping to help another was exactly the kind of thing she would do.

Or did he interrupt her run and murder her somewhere deep in the forest before finding her car and stealing her wallet? Perhaps he thought that to take her car would make him too visible to the authorities when he wished to stay out of sight, and that is why he limited his theft to just her wallet. He knew the area, he could find places a body could be hidden, never to be discovered. Eaton remains a serious suspect in this case, even though he will probably never face trial for any attack on Amy.

But although Amy is now considered long dead, her memory lives on. She has featured in TV documentaries and in numerous podcasts. 'Amy Wroe Bechtel was an accomplished athlete; she was very sharp; she was community orientated in Lander,' explained one podcaster, Scott Fuller (who runs the County 10 Podcast). 'She was pretty great at anything she did.'

While interest in her case remains, the small chance exists that somebody may come forward and offer a morsel that opens up her story. It is a remote, possibly forlorn hope. But a hope, nonetheless. And perhaps that is the dichotomy of situations such as Amy's.

Even twenty-two years on from the last time anybody saw Amy Wroe Bechtel alive, her disappearance causes daily distress to some. Primarily among these people is her mother.

'A part of me Is realistic and I'm aware that she is probably not alive. I have learned to live with the fact that Amy is gone. But I have not accepted it and I will not until I know what happened,' she said.

In 2012 it seemed as though the police might make a breakthrough in what was now a longstanding cold case. The Fremont County Sheriff's Office had received a tip which they thought worthy of further investigation. Detective Zerga refused to give details at the time, and soon news dried up as whatever line of enquiry was being followed disappeared, like the subject of its concern, down some deep unidentifiable abyss.

And that is one of the tragedies with crimes of this kind. It is not just the fear, the sorrow, the grief of what has happened that grinds those closest to victims down.

It is the hope as well.

The Loop Road which runs just outside Lander, from Bruce's Parking Area to Frye Lake.

The evidence found was so thin as to be effectively non-existent. A footstep which might, or might not, have belonged to Amy but which was in any case damaged during the efforts made by volunteers to find her. A pen which might have been similar to one Amy owned, or then again, might not. It depended on who was speaking. When tragedies occur, people do everything they can to help. Sometimes that includes stretching the truth with the best of intentions but the worst of impacts.

THE DISAPPEARANCE OF ROBIN GRAHAM

JESS DILLARD

In the wee morning hours of November 15, 1970, Robin Graham's car broke down on a Los Angeles freeway. Frustrated, she found a call box and requested that an emergency operator with the California Highway Patrol get in touch with her parents to let them know she'd run out of gas.

The call was answered by Graham's little sister, who passed the information along to her parents when they came home about a half hour later. Immediately, Graham's parents hopped in their car and drove to the location their daughter had indicated. Her car was exactly where she'd said it would be, on the shoulder of the southbound Hollywood Freeway, close to Vermont Avenue and the Santa Monica offramp.

But the car was empty and locked, with no note attached. Their daughter – 18 years old, fair-skinned and 5'6" tall, with brown eyes and long brown hair – was nowhere to be found.

The help of a stranger

Robin Graham was born on June 22, 1952, in Los Angeles. With her younger sister and her parents, Marvin and Beverly Graham, she grew up in the Silverlake-Los Feliz area of the city, in a house on Lemoyne Street. After graduating in June of 1970 from John Marshall High School, Graham had just started attending Pierce College, in Woodland Hills, and had found herself a part-time position working at a Hollywood branch of Pier 1 Imports.

In fact, Graham was dropped off at her boyfriend's car in the store's parking lot shortly before she went missing. That night, she'd been hanging out with a group of friends, and at around 1:45 a.m., they'd delivered her back to the car she'd left at work a few hours earlier.

She was last seen at around 2:00 a.m., on the side of the freeway – wearing a red blouse, a pair of jeans, red clog shoes, and a dark blue corduroy jacket, clutching a leather purse. California Highway Patrol officers reported seeing the young woman beside her car, and had stopped several times to speak with her and make sure she was alright –

however, when they drove by and saw her for the last time, she'd been busy talking to a young man they didn't recognize, who was leaning in the front driver's side window.

He was described as a dark haired, white man, approximately 5'8", whom officers guessed to be in his mid-twenties. He was dressed in bell bottom trousers and a white turtle neck top. Parked just behind Graham's car was a late 1950s model Chevrolet Corvette C1 hardtop, which appeared to be either pale blue or green with primer. According to the highway patrol officers, they chose not to stop when they observed her conversing with the young man – they'd simply assumed he was a family member who had come to help after they'd placed the call to her home.

Now, however, it has been determined that this young man was likely involved with Robin Graham's disappearance, and the official policy of the California Highway Patrol has been updated to further ensure that women who find themselves broken down on the freeway will be safe and protected in similar circumstances. The policy now directs officers to remain with female motorists in distress.

An initial report indicated that Graham had left the scene voluntarily with the young man in his Corvette after successfully starting her car, but when the officer who made the report was requisitioned, he admitted that while he had seen the two interacting on the side of the road, he hadn't actually observed them leaving together.

Robin Graham's disappearance was investigated by detectives who worked in the Rampart Division of the Los Angeles Police Department, who determined that the case could possibly have been linked to several similar disappearances that had taken place in the area over the previous two years.

The wrong place for car trouble

In May of 1969, an Israeli-born student attending San Fernando Valley State College named Rose Tashman went missing after she pulled over on the Hollywood Freeway – just a few miles from the location of Graham's car – to deal with a flat tire. Tashman, whose family had moved to the U.S. just seven years earlier, was headed home from Van Nuys, where she'd been at the home of a friend studying for an upcoming test.

While she was driving back to her house in Hollywood, the tire on Tashman's 1965 beige Mustang went flat, and she pulled over at around 2 a.m. to try and fix it. The next day, her abandoned car was located along the Hollywood Freeway, close to the Highway Avenue off-ramp. The left tire was still flat, and flares had been set out around the vehicle.

It appeared that someone else had pulled over to offer Tashman some "help" – but her body was found at approximately 6 p.m. that evening. She'd been left, nude, in a brush-filled ravine just off Mulholland Drive. A medical examiner's report revealed that nine hours before her body was found, Tashman had been strangled and raped.

Just a few months before Graham's disappearance, in January of 1970, a woman named Cindy Lee Mellin went missing. While she was never found, her car was – and it was discovered with a flat tire.

The 19 year old, who worked as a clerk at the Broadway Department Store, was last spotted at the Buenaventura Shopping Centre. At approximately 9:40 p.m., Mellin was seen standing next to her vehicle in the facility's parking lot while an unidentified Caucasian man – between 30 and 40 years old – was trying to change the car's rear tire.

When Mellin never came home that night, her father went to the shopping mall to investigate the very next morning. At around 7 a.m., he arrived in the parking lot and discovered his daughter's car still on the bumper jack, with the spare tire tossed to the side. It appeared, from subsequent investigation, that the flat tire had resulted from a puncture hole – likely made with a sharp tool while she was in the shopping centre, working, earlier that day.

That March, another woman endured a terrifying encounter with a "good Samaritan" along a stretch of highway in the Modesto area. The evening of March 20, 1970, 22 year old Kathleen Johns was on her way to the San Francisco bay area to visit her mother, who had fallen ill. Headed from her home in San Bernardino, Johns had only made it as far as Modesto when a man pulled up behind her and began flashing his headlights.

Once Johns had pulled over, the man approached her vehicle and said that he'd noticed her rear wheel was loose – he'd seen it wobbling as he was driving along behind her. Not to worry, he told her, he'd tighten the lug nuts and get her safely back on the road. Johns was grateful – her ten month old daughter Jennifer was in the car, and she was seven months pregnant.

According to Johns, the man returned with a tool in hand and got to work fixing her tire. She said she heard him doing something by the wheel, and when he was finished, she said thank you and pulled out from her parking spot to head back down the highway. However, Johns had only managed to drive a few feet before the tire the man had "worked" on fell off completely.

The helpful stranger was still close by, so he backed up and got out of his vehicle to take another look at Johns' tire. He told her only one lug nut was left on the wheel, but that he could give her a ride to a nearby service station to call for some help.

"But instead of going to the station, he left the highway and drove around side roads for two hours, until shortly after midnight," read a newspaper article published about the incident. "She said he said hardly anything and did not threaten her or her baby."

After passing by several gas stations without stopping, Johns was getting increasingly uncomfortable with the situation. Along a Modesto back road, Johns told her captor that she was going to be sick, and asked him to pull over. Once the vehicle had slowed, she said she "jumped out of the car, with the baby in her arms."

She darted into a nearby field, where she crouched down and hid with baby Jennifer while the man grabbed a flashlight and began searching the area. When another truck turned onto the road, he gave up and headed back to his vehicle – giving Johns the opportunity to flag down a passing motorist and catch a ride to the local police station to make a report.

According to a newspaper article, the officer she reported the incident to, Sgt. McNatt, said, "he had just quieted her hysterical crying when she saw the Zodiac killer drawing on a wall poster."

"That's the man, that's the man!" she shouted. "That's the man that attacked me!"

McNatt believed her – Johns had been able to get several "good looks" at whoever had abducted her, especially when he'd walked out in front of the headlights of her car.

However, when police went out to investigate the area where Johns had left her vehicle, they found that it had been "totally burned." According to the newspaper article, the car was located at Byrd Road and Highway 132 – near where Johns said she'd stopped when her wheel had initially come loose. Peculiarly, whoever had burned the vehicle had taken the time to not only reattach the tire to the car, but had also moved it back to that original location.

In 1971, on March 16, a 17 year old girl named Lisa Smith disappeared while hitchhiking in Santa Rosa, California. She was last seen on Hearn Avenue, and is thought to have been attempting to reach her home in Petaluma, California. Her body has never been found.

Just more than a year later, on April 20, 1972, a young female driver pulled over on the Ventura Freeway in Agoura, California, to change a flat tire. While Ernestine Terello's abandoned car was eventually located, there was no trace of her on the scene. And only five days later, on April 25, 1972, a 20 year old Hawaiian woman named Jeanette Kamahele went missing while she was hitchhiking on Highway 101 in Santa Rosa, California. The last sighting of Kamahele was on the Cotati on ramp, where she was waiting for a friend to come and get her.

Instead, Kamahele left with a Caucasian male, between the ages of 20 and 30, with Afro-style hair. He pulled over in a pick up truck, a faded 1970 to 1972 model Chevrolet, and Kamahele took her leather purse and got in. She's never been seen since.

The very next month, on the Circle X Boy Scout Ranch in the Santa Monica Mountains, Terello's body was discovered – fully-clothed, wearing more than $2,000 worth of jewelry. According to theories presented by investigators, Terello was likely killed by someone who had offered to "help" her with the flat.

Another disappearance, this time in 1975, had details in common with Graham's, as well. Mona Jean Gallegos, a young woman of Hispanic descent, vanished while driving down an El Monte freeway. After leaving a friend's house in Alhambra at approximately 1 a.m., Gallegos was headed down the San Bernardino Freeway, on her way back to her home in Covina.

Her car was found pulled over on the highway, close to Santa Anita Avenue, locked with the gas tank empty. A 24 hour gas station was located just off the ramp near where her car had stalled, so detectives theorized that someone had likely stopped and offered her a ride to pick up some gas.

Her skeletal remains were discovered approximately six months later, in a ravine in Riverside – but other than the fact that her body was finally found, detectives believe Gallegos' case is nearly identical to Graham's. Several other victims who disappeared along the freeways in the area were eventually found dead in the Hollywood Hills – however, Graham, like Cindy Lee Mellin, Lisa Smith, and Jeanette Kamahele, hasn't been seen since.

Speculation and far-fetched theories

Months after Robin Graham went missing, another woman went to police and told them that her car had stalled along the same freeway

– and a Corvette had pulled up behind her. The man behind the wheel had come over to check on her, she said, claiming to be an off duty detective and offering to help get her car started. According to the woman, he left after she refused his offer, but she later identified him as Bruce Davis – one of a number of men suspected of being the Zodiac killer.

In the late 1970s, a serial killer known only as the Zodiac killer kept all of California in a state of terror for several years. Although the identity of the murderer has never been determined, he remains a suspect in a number of unsolved murders and disappearances from the area at that time. There has also been speculation linking the Zodiac killer to Charles Manson, who was sent to death row for ordering the killings of the LaBianca family and residents at the home of actress Sharon Tate.

If Bruce Davis was the same man who had been spotted under the hood of Robin Graham's car – the man she later left with – it's possible he had something to do with her disappearance. And, if Davis is truly the Zodiac killer, it's likely that Robin Graham was one of his earliest victims, although there is still no evidence that points to foul play.

The Zodiac killer was known to kill on or around the full moon, which lines up with Graham's disappearance. And, considering so many other young brunettes vanished in similar circumstances along nearby roadways, it certainly seems as though offering "help" to women in need was an easy way for a predator to gain a potential victim's trust.

However, the main difference that makes Graham's disappearance stand apart from the murders committed by the Zodiac killer is that detectives have never been able to locate Graham's body.

The Zodiac killer was a widely known serial murderer who was recognized for how blatantly he flaunted his kills – he wasn't the type to be discreet about committing murder, and likely would never have hidden a body so well that it would never been found. Not only did he leave his victims' bodies out where anyone could see them, he was also known for frequently sending letters to the police and media outlets, graphically describing and even bragging about the women he'd killed.

Speculation has also been made linking Graham's case to the Santa Rosa Hitchhiker Murders. These killings happened around the same time, in a similar area, and appear to have been committed by the same perpetrator. The remains of the six girls identified as victims of the Santa Rosa Hitchhiker predator were all discovered in the Hollywood Hills, and all appear to have been between the ages of 12 to 20.

According to some familiar with the cases, the Santa Rosa Hitchhiker abductor seems to match the description of the man who was seen with Graham just before she went missing. And, while Santa Rosa is a fair distance from Los Angeles, Highway 101 provides a straight shot directly into the city.

On May 22, 1971, an "unidentified deceased" was found by a group of kids hanging out in a ravine located at the base of a cliff in Granada Hills, Los Angeles County. Although the skeletal remains are estimated to belong to a female, approximately 5'8" and between the ages of 16 and 20, an official identification was not possible – leading some to speculate that this could be what is left of the body of Robin Graham.

"A major brush fire had gone through this area during September 1970, and there have been heavy rains and an earthquake since that time," states the NAMUS entry for the case.

Bad Samaritans

Concerns had been raised about attacks on female motorists in the area in the years leading up to Graham's disappearance. A pattern of attacks on women driving on roadways around Van Nuys in 1967 led local newspapers and police to advise the public to be aware of the situation.

"Valley women yesterday were warned by police to be on the lookout for a man who has assaulted three women this month," read an article published by an area newspaper. "West Valley detectives Lou Netza and Sgt. Don Zellers said the women were attacked by a man who got his victims to stop driving after indicating something was wrong with their cars."

According to the article, this assailant had been described by the women as a man in his mid-20s, approximately 6'1" and of medium build, with dark hair. Sgt. Zellers said he had been driving different cars in all three incidents, making him more difficult for concerned drivers to spot. One vehicle was believed to be a little white sports car; another, possibly a late model Plymouth of some kind. The third vehicle was unknown, as no description had been provided.

The first attack was reported to police on November 8, 1967. A woman informed police that she and another female had been driving to work in the morning when a man pulled up and motioned for them to get off the road. She stopped near Nordhoff St. and Topanga Canyon Blvd. at around 5:20 a.m., after the man seemed to be indicating that she was about to lose a wheel from her vehicle.

"The man pretended to check the wheel, then suggested the car would have to be towed away," the article stated.

He drove the female passenger to a nearby gas station and instructed her to wait for an available attendant, who would be able to arrange for a tow truck which she could then direct back to her friend's vehicle. Meanwhile, he returned to the stranded driver and proposed that he take the car for a quick test drive.

"He drove the woman to a dead end street and began beating her," read the article. "He took an old bedspread, which he found in the car, placed it over her face and threatened to kill her if she screamed."

Once he'd finished beating her, he forced her out of the vehicle and ordered her to go walk into a field off the side of the road. He took off in her car, which he returned to the location where he'd taken it. After parking her vehicle, he got back into his own car and left the scene.

Other reports were filed by multiple women who had been through similar assaults – after alerting the drivers to some kind of automotive issue, he would offer to help or give them a lift to a service station.

Some women reported that, while he seemed suspicious and vaguely threatening, he never went through with a physical attack. Others weren't as fortunately, although none of the women were seriously harmed.

However, after committing a number of assaults, the man seemed to vanish. Since he was never arrested – or even identified – some have connected this string of attacks to the incident with Kathleen Johns, and the disappearances of women like Cindy Lee Mellin, Lisa Smith, Jeanette Kamahele, and Robin Graham.

Then, in the fall of 1968, a familiar incident was reported in Berkeley. Two young women were walking together along Telegraph Avenue when a strange man drove up next to them and asked if he could offer them a ride. Pointing to the Volkswagen Bug they had parked just ahead, they turned him down and continued on their way to a nearby café. After spending about 45 minutes inside the building, the women headed back to their vehicle – but when they tried to drive away, they discovered that the car wouldn't start.

As the women attempted to get the car running, a car pulled up next to them. The man who had asked if they needed a ride about an hour before was, for some reason, still driving around the neighbourhood, and again offered his help. This time, they accepted his assistance. As he helped the women push the vehicle away from traffic, another man showed up to lend a hand.

Apparently, this set the first man off. He began cursing at the second man and stormed away. The second man popped the hood of the VW Bug and started looking for what might be causing a problem – and quickly found it. A wire had been purposely pulled out, likely by the first man while the two women were enjoying a snack shortly after he spoke to them.

"Early winter nightfall, and late holiday shopping, makes women who drive alone particularly vulnerable," warned Long Beach Detective Ken Schack in a newspaper article about an increase of attacks on

Southland women around the same time. "Too often, the victim's mind is on her shopping, rather than her safety."

He advised women who can't avoid driving alone in the evenings to keep their car doors locked and their windows up, particularly on the passenger side. Vulnerable women should also plan their routes along well-lit, frequently used roads, and stop for traffic lights in the center lane whenever possible.

"Still looking for you."

Seventeen years after Robin Graham's disappearance, an ad showed up in the classified section of the Los Angeles Times.

"Dearest Robin," it read. "You ran out of gas on the Hollywood Frwy. A man in a Corvette pulled over to help. You've not been seen of since. It's been 17 years, but it's always just yesterday. Still looking for you (signed) THE ECHO PARK DUCKS."

The ad immediately caught the attention of a disc jockey with KFI in Los Angeles named Geoff Edwards. He read the mysterious posting on the air, hoping to find out more about the circumstances around the bizarre classified ad.

"It sounded so romantic," Edwards told the Los Angeles Times a few weeks later, in December of 1987. "I wondered if anyone knew what it was all about, and I got all kinds of calls and mail. Someone even wondered if the message was a clue to the killing."

The Graham family also happened across the ad, which, according to Robin Graham's mother Beverly, was quite surprising.

"One of our daughters saw it," she said. "The funny thing is, she never looks at the personal ads. But this one day..."

After some investigating, it was revealed that the author of the post was a 36 year old computer operator by the name of Al Medrano. Medrano, another long time resident of Echo Park, was an old friend of Graham's who was still living in the area. According to Medrano, this was the first time he'd ever placed an ad of that nature, in an effort to remember his old friend.

"Well, it occurred to me that November 15 (the day of Graham's disappearance) fell on the same day (Sunday) this year as it did in 1970," Medrano explained in an interview with the Los Angeles Times. "And I just wanted to show she wasn't forgotten."

He also provided some context to account for the bizarre sign off he'd chosen to use in his post.

"She and I were both from Echo Park, and the Echo Park Ducks was a group of our friends, back then," he said. "I wanted to make it from all of us."

Although it had been seventeen years, at that time, since her daughter had gone missing, Beverly Graham told the Los Angeles Times that she's never given up on the case – despite a complete lack of evidence to support any possible theory.

"It's strange," she said. "It happened right in the middle of the city, but there never really were any clues. Maybe it will turn something up," she added, referring to the classified ad placed by Medrano. "We still live with that hope."

MURDER IN TEXAS : THE TRUE STORY OF RHONDA JOHNSON & SHARON SHAW

JAMIE FOSTER

Rhonda Johnson and Sharon Shaw were two teenage girls murdered in 1971. But despite having had their lives taken so long ago, their case is still not satisfactorily solved. It's a story that involves not just two girls being murdered so young, but a potentially innocent man imprisoned for over twenty years, a corrupt police force, a serial killer, and perhaps the wider context of the Texas Killing Fields murders.

The story of the twists and turns involved in finding justice for the two girls continues on until today. Michael Lloyd Self, the man who some believe to have been wrongly imprisoned for the murder of the two girls, has since died in prison of cancer. Because of his passing, and the difficulty that investigators have found in unearthing new evidence, it seemed unlikely that the full story will ever come out.

But not long ago, a revelation and a startling confession have brought Johnson and Shaw's murders back into the limelight. Perhaps, at last, their families can discover the truth of their real killers.

Who were Rhonda Renee Johnson and Sharon Shaw?

Sharon Lynn Shaw was born in Mobile, Alabama to Hoyt Shaw and Mary Ann Collins on August 11th, 1957. Rhonda was born in Houston, Texas to Charles Johnson Sr. and Betty Huey on December 16th, 1956. Not much is known of their early lives, although by 1971 they were living next to one another in Webster, Texas, and were good friends.

Both girls had finished with school for the year and were enjoying their time off together. The day of their disappearance began like many others that summer, with a day out on a pleasant morning. It was August 4th, 1971 and Johnson and Shaw wanted to take a day trip to Galveston, to Wix Ski School, and to visit Doug's Surf and Dive Shop which was nearby. The area also had a Dairy Queen and a popular swimming school, making it very popular with the teenagers of the surrounding area. Given that it was summer, the girls would most likely have preferred to stay all day, but had promised their parents that they would be home by 1pm.

They hitched a ride with a family friend, who took them on the 30 mile journey to Galveston. Unfortunately for the girls' parents, that morning would be the last that they would ever see of their children.

The afternoon came and went, and the girls didn't call home to explain their absence. After they missed dinner that night, their parents began to call their friends to see if they'd heard from them, and called the neighbor who had given them a ride. None of their friends had heard a thing, and the last their neighbor had seen was when the girls had been dropped off at the skiing school and surf club. The girls were soon reported missing by their parents, who went in person to the local police department.

According to Raymond Wix, the owner of Wix Ski School, the girls didn't stay long there that day. In conversation with the Webster Police Department, he had told them that they had headed off after being told that the ski boats weren't running that day due to choppy waters. That was the last that we can say with certainty about the girls' day.

It was in August that the pair crossed paths with the man who would end their lives, but it wasn't until the beginning of 1972 that the girls' bodies were found. Just after the New Year, two young men went fishing near Webster, Texas, their hometown. They came across a skull floating in the marsh, and one of the men wrapped it up in a towel, stowed it away and took it home. After sharing their find with the Harris County Sherriff, the skull was eventually identified as belonging to the missing Rhonda Johnson.

This triggered a large scale search of Taylor Lake and the Bayou, which despite its size took until February 17th to find any more evidence. That day, another skull was found in a nearby drainage ditch, and soon more bones were found. They were identified as belonging to both girls.

Michael Lloyd Self tried and convicted

While the girls' bodies were discovered in early January, it was only in late May the same year that progress began on their case. The city council hired a new police chief that month, Don Morris, who brought with him a new assistant chief, Tommy Deal. Eager that they be seen to be doing something on such a large crime for a small town, the pair acted on a tip they'd received about local man Michael Lloyd Self.

Self was, admittedly, a sex offender known locally who had already been arrested multiple times in 'Peeping Tom' incidents. It was Morris and Deal themselves who visited Self at his place of work, a gas station, where Self was working night shifts at the time. They questioned him on the topic of the 'two girls'- the officers, of course, referring to Johnson and Shaw. Self, however, believed them to mean his estranged wife and new girlfriend, and having been confused went to the police station later that day to clear the matter.

Upon his arrival, he was again questioned about Johnson and Shaw, this time being shown their photographs and interrogated on his connection to them. Self admitted to recognising them, and unfortunately for him, that seemed to be enough evidence for the new chief: he was arrested then and there on the charge of their murders.

Since he was now officially detained at the station- he had, after all, only arrived voluntarily that morning- Self's interrogation could now begin in earnest. Morris and Deal claimed that their suspicions rested on evidence that they had obtained, and urged him to confess. According to Jerry Mitchell, another officer at the police station that day, Self appeared calm and rational throughout the early stages of his questioning, clearly expecting any second that the officers would realise they had the wrong man.

He continued to deny the crimes as the morning wore on, but according to Self, the interrogations became continually more threatening and violent. Morris held him up against the wall, jabbed him with his nightstick, and even threatened to shoot him were he to carry on denying the crimes. Finally, Self had had enough: he wrote out his confession. He would later claim that Morris told him what to write, even forcing him to rewrite his confession several times over, a claim echoed once more by Jerry Mitchell.

During his time in court, Michael claimed that his confession had been forced out of him by the two officers interrogating him. These concerns were quickly dismissed, since after all, which murderer doesn't deny the charges against them?

Self's Confession: Details and Inconsistencies

It is easy to see why a jury or a prosecutor might be taken in by the confession, were they to consider the case 'open and shut' and not give it enough thought. It is particularly detailed with regards to the murders. Self first describes how he picked up Rhonda as he saw her walking along the road, turning around to pick her up in his car. They then drove to the Nassau Bay Yacht Club, where Rhonda found her friend Sharon. He claimed that he provided them with beer, offered them marijuana which they declined, and drove around the Clear Lake area 'feel[ing] good and getting loud.'

As the night wore on, Self's version of events is that Sharon had been hanging out of the window 'hollering at everybody and shooting peace signs at them' as he drove. Since neither of the girls wanted to go home, he claimed they went down to Clear Lake where he tried to assault Rhonda, which she rejected. Since Sharon was out of the car, Self continued assaulting her, and at her continued protests he became angry and hit both Sharon and Rhonda over the head with a Coke bottle repeatedly until they were both unconscious.

He goes on to describe how he drove the girls to an abandoned, dead end road, stripped them of their clothes and dumped their bodies in the Bayou.

Reading back the confession that Self may or may not have been forced to write, it is at least easy to spot several glaring, obvious mistakes. Perhaps the worst is that according to his confession, Self disposed of the girls' bodies more than twenty miles from where they were actually found. Both of the girls were found with their clothes on, not stripped as Self had claimed. Even the method by which he confessed to having murdered Johnson and Shaw was incorrect according to the coroner's report, with Self claiming to have strangled the girls, but their bodies showing no such marks.

Moreover, Sharon's family dispute the confession since it mentions Self picking up the young girl from her family home, which they deny. The confession also states that Self and the two girls were in Webster at 9pm, whereas eyewitnesses disagree and place the two girls- alone- in Galveston instead. The written confession is even further discredited by Self's later verbal confessions, which contradict several key points. For instance, Self repeated his claim during a polygraph test taken three days after his initial arrest that he stripped the girls before dumping their bodies, when they were in fact found with their clothes on.

The story only continues to get stranger. Two weeks after Self was first arrested, while the officers were still building the case against him, he was actually taken from jail by two deputies. They had told Self that they were going to buy him dinner. In fact, they took him out of town to the locations which Self had mentioned in his confessions to take pictures of him as a sort of third and final confession. These photos were even presented in court as evidence.

This episode is mentioned in the court records of Self's appeal. There, the scene is painted as Self agreeing to show the two deputies the various locations involved in the murder. First, the group went to the Sizzler Steak House, where Self said he picked up Rhonda (contradicting his claim that he had picked her up on El Camino Real, a nearby street, where she had been walking). According to this testimony, after picking up Sharon they then went to a Jack in the Box restaurant. The fact that this confession had been so different to his previous one, however, did not constitute enough of a problem for either confession to be inadmissible according to the court records of Self's appeal case.

Time passes by

After Self's conviction, justice did appear to have been done. Trust in the police was higher than it is today; if a man had been arrested, tried, and convicted of a crime then the case was, quite simply, closed. Self, for his part, never gave in. He continually appealed the case and applied for parole, beginning taking the case to an appeals court just a year after his first imprisonment.

According to the court records, Self complained on several grounds. First, he claimed that the evidence presented at his first trial was 'insufficient to sustain his conviction', mostly due to his claim that his confession was forced, but also because the photos taken at the various locations relevant to the case shouldn't have been admitted as evidence.

Unfortunately, each time Self applied for parole, or put his case up for appeal, he was unsuccessful. In the eyes of the law there was little reason to overturn the ruling. Self's first confession did contain some errors, but was also correct on several points, particularly that the bodies were disposed of and found in water. At appeal, the judge decided that enough of the confession corroborated with material evidence to uphold the previous verdict.

While Self's protests had been dismissed, the case still seemed to some to be too flimsy to have justified the certainty of a seventy year sentence. Like many similar cases before his, Self's case was eventually dramatized as part of the TV show, Unresolved Mysteries. David Coburn, a local investigator interviewed in the episode, actually backed up Self's story of Morris' mistreatment of him during his interrogation. Coburn claimed that he had seen Morris' brutality first hand during another interrogation the year before. The show raised the same questions as Self had done, but of course left it to the viewer to decide as to whether he truly was guilty or not.

Morris and Deal's Motives: The Texas Killing Fields

The show also raised the question of why, exactly, Morris and Deal had been so eager to arrest Self on such little evidence. In all of their efforts to extract repeated confessions from the defendant, it certainly seemed that they must have had their reasons. First, Self was well known locally for his sexual misdemeanors. For the city, it would make their lives a lot easier to finally put Self away for a longer sentence. It also made sense for the new chief to make it obvious that he was hard on crime. A new chief not addressing one of the largest and most shocking cases in Webster history would certainly give a bad first impression.

Last, but certainly not least, is the fact that the area had seen an unnaturally large number of murders from the start of the 1970s, which we today call the Texas Killing Fields murders. If Johnson and Shaw really were victims of the same serial killer as the other murders in the area, they were some of the very first to be killed. However, by the time they were discovered, five other girls' bodies had been found in the local area.

Whether law enforcement at the time would have recognised that these murders were perhaps the work of a repeat killer, they would at least have been aware of the spate of local killings, and been desperate to pin the crime on somebody. This, perhaps, was part of the reason why Morris and Deal were more eager than they should have been to try to pin those crimes on Self. At the very least, newspaper clippings from the time of the investigation reveal the public concern over previous missing persons' cases, as well as the deaths of many other young girls from the area. In a copy of The Odessa American from June 10th 1970, the author reveals that Self was suspected to perhaps have had a hand in the many other recent local murders.

The two girls were far from the last victims, however, as the Texas Killing Fields murders continued through the 1980s and 1990s, some even coming after the turn of the century. Almost every victim has been between the ages of 12 and 17, and every victim has been a young girl or woman. In total, at least 30 bodies have been found all within a 25 acre area just off I-45. Even aside from the discovered bodies, many more local girls have gone missing and are featured on websites like The Charley Project, a site dedicated to tracking down missing persons. All of this has led some to believe that the murders must be the work of a serial killer.

They certainly fit the bill: all around the same area, the vast majority of the victims fitting the same description, and a relatively steady pace of killings through the years all suggest the work of one lone actor. The only real argument against the idea is the fact that the killer must somehow have remained at large for so long, despite leaving such an obvious trail. If the murder of Johnson and Shaw really were part of the Texas Killing Fields murders- and given that the murders were often of pairs of young girls around their age, it would seem very likely- then Self could not have been their killer, since the murders continued for long after he was incarcerated.

A Twist in the Tale

Whether the Texas Killing Fields murders were the acts of a lone serial killer, or how he must be innocent if Johnson and Shaw were two victims of that same killer, was irrelevant to Michael Lloyd Self. Despite all of his protestations, appeals, and parole hearings, he remained in prison. It was only in 1998 that any development in this seemingly long-dead case came about. Edward Harold Bell was already in prison, after a manhunt that spanned the globe. He had been on the run since 1978, after the attempted assault of a group of children and the murder of a Marine, Larry Dickens, who had attempted to intervene.

The murder was especially brutal. It had taken place in a normal, suburban street; Bell had been coasting around in his car, searching for girls. Finding a group of young teenagers, he had stopped his car and jumped out, not wearing anything below the waist. Dickens, a local resident, noticed what was happening and attempted to intervene. Unfortunately for him, Dickens didn't like being interrupted.

He went back to his car, picked up a pistol and began shooting. Larry struggled back to the garage, where his mother had been watching the scene, and collapsed in her arms. Bell didn't stop shooting. When he ran out of bullets in his pistol, he went back to his truck to exchange it for his rifle, and carried on.

Bell would have been guaranteed life in prison for the brutal murder, but skipped bail and went on the run for 15 years. In 1984 he be was identified as part of a failed burglary in Texas, but still managed to avoid the police before finally being tracked down in Panama in 1993. Upon his eventual capture, he was finally convicted of the murder of Dickens and received 70 years in prison. Bell's murder of Dickens, too, was featured on Unresolved Mysteries; curiously, Matthew McConaughey caught his first big break on TV playing the role of Larry.

His connection to the Johnson and Shaw case was completely unknown before he confessed not just to their murders, but to the murder of eleven girls in total in the 1970s. The frankly disturbing letters were sent to prosecutors for both Harris County and Galveston County way back in 1998, but were kept under wraps until 2011. The letters initially claimed a tally of seven lives, but in interviews with the Houston Chronicle after their publication admitted to the total of eleven murders. In them, he claimed to have been a part of a government brainwashing program that forced him to assault, rape, and kill young girls.

Who Was Edward Harold Bell?

According to the Houston Chronicle, Bell had a 'normal' early life, 'even exemplary'. A boy scout who went on to earn a degree from Texas A&M, he made his living first as a licensed diver- where he met his wife- before settling as a travelling pharmaceutical salesman in West Texas. On the surface, he seemed like a normal man, with a normal job, and a happy wife and family.

According to Bell himself, however, his childhood was not idyllic. His family were always on the move since his father worked as a gauger at small oil fields across Texas, earning plenty of money to provide for his wife and son but forcing them to live an itinerant lifestyle. Not just this, but Bell also claimed that his father was excessively violent towards his family: in Bell's own words, 'My father thought if he beat you real bad, it would send chemicals into your bloodstream.' Bell fathered three children of his own over the years- but what his family didn't know was that he was leading a sordid double life.

Bell's crimes began much the same way as Self's had done: Bell progressed from peeping tom incidents, to masturbating in public and exposing himself to girls around Texas. According to the Chronicle, he was apprehended committing public indecencies at least twelve times, from Lubbock to Houston; his targets, teenage girls, often in pairs, but always unaccompanied by adults. More often than not, he managed to avoid prosecution or arrest for his actions. He began- at least, he was first caught- in 1968, exposing himself to teenage girls in the town of Sudan. Police and court records show that he continued on and off until at least 1978, the year he murdered Larry Dickens for interrupting an episode of his flashing.

Bell was in and out of mental institutions for a large part of that decade, on referral from court. He somehow didn't receive a single jail sentence for any of his sexual crimes, something which most likely wouldn't happen today. If he had been appropriately dealt with by the police for his previous crimes, the life of Larry Dickens could have been saved. In fairness to the police, however, his violent outburst was entirely unprecedented.

What Happened Next?

It would seem that at last, justice could have been done. Through all the years, Self had maintained his innocence, continued to claim that his confession had been forced, and that despite knowing the girls he had not been involved in their murders. Bell was a known murderer, already in prison, and provided remarkably accurate details with relevance to several missing persons cases in his letters. It would seem that given this detail, and Bell's prior crimes, that his confessions would force prosecutors to re-open the case and for Self's version of events, perhaps, to be reheard and finally believed.

All of this was not to be. As is so often the case with decades-old missing persons cases- in particular cases that seemed as closed as this- the new evidence wasn't treated with the interest it should have been. Astonishingly, Galveston County refused to present the letters to a jury for their consideration, and even worse, Harris County actually lost the letters altogether. Self remained in prison, unaware that a confession had even been made.

One of the prosecutors for Galveston County stated to the Houston Chronicle that he "...didn't believe we had sufficient evidence that we could proceed to grand jury with, and without getting into specifics, that's the decision that had to be made, no matter the temptations to proceed otherwise ... It wasn't for a lack of effort." In fairness to the prosecutors, the evidence to reopen a case of murder- particularly one that already, in the eyes of the law, has been settled- has to be very compelling, and perhaps the confession of a man known to be mentally unstable is not enough. After all, serial killers have been known to confess to crimes they may not have committed to gain infamy, or recapture the spotlight long after their conviction.

It was only two years later that Michael Lloyd Self died in prison, of cancer. If he really was innocent- and on the balance of probabilities, it seems that he may have been- then he will never see justice for his unlawful incarceration, which lasted a total twenty seven years before his death.

As for Bell, he remains in prison. He received 70 years for the inexplicably brutal murder of Larry Dickens, and so any sentence received for the murders of Johnson and Shaw- not to mention the other girls he claimed to have killed in the same letters- would be irrelevant. Bell was in his late 70s at the time of writing, and will die in prison.

The Johnson and Shaw cases are still, officially, the crimes of Michael Lloyd Self, and the case remains closed. Since Bell's letters were received by county prosecutors, no new evidence has come to light; the letters and accompanying information were not considered enough to reopen the case then, and aren't considered enough now. And due to Bell's refusal to co-operate with police, it seems unlikely that any new information on his potential part in the murders will ever be revealed.

BONUS STORY :

Texarkana has always been an unusual place. On the east, you have Texarkana, Arkansas, a small town by any other measurement, yet home to the largest population in Miller County. To the west lies Texarkana, Texas, located in rural Bowie County and lucky enough to have its very own Wal-Mart. Together these twin cities make up what is simply referred to as "Texarkana."

Texarkana is a dusty town, built on a foundation of competing railroads and a Mexican border dispute in the 1800s. The town laid low for the next several years, sending off its sons to fight World War I and then II, and welcoming them back home for better or for worse. But no one in Texarkana was prepared for the national attention that came in the spring of 1946. On February 22nd, 1946, a masked serial killer, dubbed the "Phantom Killer" by the *Texarkana Gazette*'s Calvin Sutton, began terrorizing young couples on the town's secluded country roads.

Today, if you search the Internet for information on Texarkana and its morbid history, you will likely be redirected to pages on *The Town That Dreaded Sundown* and its Arkansan producer, Charles B. Pierce. In 1977, decades after the last murders, this film joined the ranks of *Halloween* and *The Texas Chainsaw Massacre* as one of Hollywood's classic horrors, featuring countless local residents as set extras. While the film's accuracy is something to be questioned, it remains a key piece of the town's identity. Visitors can even catch a screening every Halloween at Spring Lake Park, not far from where one of the infamous murders took place.

Texarkana may have embraced its celebrity status, but eighty years ago the town was paralyzed in fear. Within a single spring, five were dead and three were wounded. All in what had previously been a quiet, friendly community.

A Masked Attacker

Just before midnight, on February 22nd, 1946, Jimmy Hollis and Mary Jeanne Larey were finishing up their date in the backseat of Hollis' father's car. Hollis, 24, and Larey, 19, had been dating for a while, but his parents expected the car (and the lovebirds) home by midnight. Throwing caution to the wind, they parked on a secluded dirt road, known as a lovers' lane, and proceeded to do what young couples will do.

The pair was soon startled by a flashlight, shining through the driver side window and blinding them to whoever stood outside. Hollis quickly composed himself and opened the door, thinking they were being interrupted by an ill-timed police patrol or a prank from some local kids, but they found themselves face-to-face with a masked man holding a gun.

Hollis continued to confront the intruder, telling him, "Fellow, you've got me mixed up with someone else. You got the wrong man." Hollis later said that the masked man muttered something like, "I don't want to kill you, so do what I say." Hollis attempted to calm the assailant, who forced the young man out of the vehicle and demanded Hollis remove his pants, gun pointed squarely at his face. Larey pleaded with Hollis to do as the man said, thinking he would not become violent if they did as he said. Instead the masked man overpowered Hollis, beating him over the head with the revolver. As Hollis lay limp on the cold ground, the attack continued until the sound of Hollis' skull cracking echoed throughout the clearing.

At this point Larey was hysterical with panic, thinking the loud crack of Hollis' broken skull was the sound of him being shot. She told the man they had no money or valuables, attempting to hand the man Hollis' wallet, but he only screamed, "Liar," at her and demanded her purse. Then the masked man told her to run toward the road. Larey ran as fast as she could, but the strange man pursued, continuing to scream, "Liar," at her as she ran.

The assailant eventually outpaced Larey, and forced her to the ground. Larey reported that the man did not rape her, but that assaulted her violent and used his gun to sexually molest her. Larey was afraid for her life, fighting against the weight of her attacker. She eventually managed to escape his grasp, rising up and telling him, "Go ahead and kill me." She then ran to a nearby house at 805 Blanton Street, where she managed to wake up the sleeping woners and pleaded for help. Shortly after, the Bowie County Sheriff, W.H. "Bill" Presley, arrived at what would be the first known Phantom Killer crime scene.

Hollis and Larey were lucky enough to survive this first attack, though they were left with plenty of physical and emotional scars to show for it. Hollis and Larey described their attacker as a tall man wearing a burlap sack with two slits cut for the eyes, though they could not agree on the man's race. Hollis believed the man was white, with tanned skin from working outdoors, while Larey insisted he was a black man because of his mannerisms and "curses." At this point, the attack was treated as a random attempted robbery, it was unknown the chaos that the Phantom Killer would bring in coming months.

The First Kill

In the early hours of March 24th, a truck driver spotted a young man asleep in an Oldsmobile parked on the side of the road. Concerned about the danger of passing traffic, the truck driver ran up to the window, hoping to wake the man and advise him of a better resting area. To the truck driver's horror, the young man was not asleep; he had been shot twice in the back of the head and sat dead in the driver's seat. In the Oldsmobile's backseat was a teenage girl wrapped in a bloody blanket, her body was completely lifeless. These young lovers were not as lucky as the Phantom Killer's first victims.

Richard Griffin, 29, was a retired Navy SeaBee on a double date with his girlfriend of six weeks, Polly Ann Moore, 17, when they pulled over on the highway to have some time alone. They had just finished up dinner with Griffin's sister and her boyfriend at a local café, and

Griffin was in no rush to return his girlfriend to her parents' house. Unfortunately, they would never make it home.

Sometime that previous night, Griffin and Moore had pulled over onto the side of the road. It is believed they were approached similarly to the Phantom Killer's first victims, with a blinding flashlight and pointed gun. There was a heavy rainfall over Texarkana that night, so no one would have been out and about to see the killings take place.

Griffin was likely killed first, with two shots from a .32 Colt revolver to the back of his head. Moore, however, had been dragged from the vehicle and sexually assaulted on the cold, wet ground by their attacker. Blood and marks littered the dirt next to the vehicle. After this horror, Moore was also shot and killed by the Phantom Killer. The assailant pulled a blanket from the car's trunk and wrapped her in it before placing her body in the backseat of the Oldsmobile. Any fingerprints and footprints left behind by the killer that night was washed away by the storm.

Griffin's pockets were found empty and turned inside out, and Moore's purse remained at the scene but was emptied of any cash. With the only apparent motive being robbery, questions still remained as to why the crime was carried out so violently. The *Texarkana Gazette*, at the insistence of the Sheriff Bill Presley, made an announcement on March 27th asking residents to not spread rumors or anything else that they did not see with their own two eyes. Despite offering a cash reward, no solid tips ever made it to the police force.

Murder in the Park

Betty Jo Booker, 15, was a straight-A student who was adored by those around her. She worked with Jerry Atkins playing saxophone for a local band, The Rhythmaires, every Saturday night at the local VFW club. On April 14th, she and Atkins, as well as the rest of their band mates, were playing one of their normal shows. Every other weekend, Atkins gave Booker a ride home alternating with a band mate named Ernie Holcomb. This night was Holcomb's night to drive her home, but Booker told Holcomb not to bother because she had a ride set up with an old classmate who was visiting, Paul Martin. Atkins never knew of this change of plans, and until he received a call the next morning he assumed Booker had left with Holcombe, as usual.

Martin's 1946 Ford Coupe was found at 6:30 the next morning by the Weaver family, who were on their way through Texarkana to Prescott, Arkansas. The keys were found still in the car's ignition. Several miles away, in Spring Lake Park, their bodies would be found. Neither the car nor their bodies were anywhere near their destination that night.

Band and classmates claimed that the two were never close to being a couple, and that Booker felt obligated to go out with Martin because of their connection at school. However, no one knows what they were doing pulled over that night, or why they were in that area of town in the first place. No matter what the true story was that night, Booker and Martin would be the Phantom Killer's third and fourth victims.

Like the previous attack, both victims were shot and killed with a .32 Colt semi-automatic revolver. And like the female targets before her, Booker had been sexually assaulted before her murder. After news of the murder was released, hundreds of Texarkana residents flooded the park, hoping to catch a glimpse of the crime scene or help the investigation.

Martin's body was found almost a mile and a half from the abandoned car. He had been shot four times and the ground surrounding his body was covered in his blood.

Booker's body would not be found until five hours later, over three miles from where the car had been found. Booker was found by the Boyd family and Ted Schoeppey, who had joined the community search party to help find the two teenage victims. Booker had been shot twice, and was found with her hand in her coat pocket.

Both bodies showed signs of a struggle against their attacker, yet their fight was unsuccessful. There was no conclusive evidence as to why their bodies were so far from their car.

Booker's missing saxophone played in the running theory of robbery as a primary motive. The police had alerts al over the area, asking people to keep an eye out for a pawned or for sale saxophone matching the serial number of Booker's, and for several months it was considered one of the best leads the authorities had on finding the killer. Unfortunately for the police, on October 24th, six months after Booker's murder, P. V. Ward and J. F. McNief found the saxophone still in its leather case, just yards from where Booker's body had been found. Ward claimed to know what it was as soon as they stumbled upon it. By the time the case and instrument were turned over to the police, the case had already been labeled closed.

A Red Herring

Public panic over the Phantom Killer was at its all-time high when Virgil and Katie Starks were attacked in their modest farmhouse just ten miles out of town. However, questions would eventually emerge over whether this was truly the work of the Phantom Killer, or if someone else was responsible for the crime.

On the quiet night of May 3[rd,] Virgil, 36, was reading the Texarkana Gazette when two gunshots burst through the front window of their ranch-style home. These bullets hit Virgil in the head, killing him instantly. Katie was lying in bed, already dressed in her nightgown, when she heard the sound of breaking glass. She headed for the living room, where her husband had been seated, only to find him slumped in his armchair, dead. She cried in fear as she reached for the phone, but the attacker shot through her lower jaw, spraying teeth fragments across the Starks kitchen.

In a state of panic and extreme pain, Katie managed to get back up to her feet. She attempted to grab her husband's gun, but was disoriented from being shot. Despite her injuries, she escaped from the house and ran for her sister's down the street. Finding the house empty, she continued to her neighbors' until she found refuge in the Prater house, where the police were finally called. When A. V. Prater answered the door, Katie simply said, "Virgil's dead," before collapsing on the ground. In the time it took for the police to arrive the killer had fled, taking no valuables or anything else of note with him.

Initially, this attack was labeled as another of the Phantom Killer's. It followed the same time pattern as his previous attacks, used a gun as the primary weapon, and targeted a couple. One of the biggest pieces of evidence connecting this attack to the Phantom Killer was a set of unfamiliar tire tracks that matched those found at the other crime scenes. Because of these similarities, many citizens of Texarkana insist that this murder and attempted assault was the Phantom Killer's final blow to the small town's community.

In November 1948, the local authorities made a different conclusion. Another man was arrested and charged with the home invasion and attack on Virgil and Katie Starks. Law enforcement referenced several reasons as to this not being the work of the Phantom Killer, including the fact that the weapon used was a .22 rifle. This change in weapon, as well as the fact this was a home invasion earlier in the evening, pointed police to consider a different suspect entirely.

The town is still home to many skeptics who believe this attack was the Phantom Killer's doing. The crime scene at the Starks home was filled with physical DNA evidence, but at the time DNA testing was only beginning to emerge in the most developed areas of the nation. A little town like Texarkana was nowhere near equipped to handle a case like this, and the DNA evidence was discarded or improperly stored for later testing. While the official stance is that the Phantom Killer was not involved in this attack, the question still haunts many in the area.

A Town In Panic

As the attacks added up, tension in the town of Texarkana grew. After the first and second attack, police forces from both states increased patrols on the town's secluded back roads. A community that had once been friendly, where front doors were never locked and neighbors were always welcome, now grew eerily quiet after sundown.

Businesses saw a decline in customers, especially those catering to the night crowd. Residents were afraid to leave home, even during the daylight, for fear they may become the next target of the Phantom Killer. However, one industry in town became a hotspot for concerned citizens – the local hardware and ammo shops.

Residents bought up guns and ammo like crazy, hoping to be able to defend themselves from the attacks. Deadbolts and other home security devices became commonplace in all the towns households, and some homeowners were even seen setting up booby traps and other contraptions to catch the killer in his tracks.

Many of the town's local high school and college boys rounded up patrol groups. These men would go out at night with baseball bats and other makeshift weapons, hoping to catch the Phantom Killer on the prowl. None of them were ever successful.

Rumors continued to spread and impair the investigations. There was constant news about someone's son being arrested for the murders, or a suspect being charged, but these rumors rarely ever revealed themselves to be true. Police were forced to perform damage control on the stories spreading around town while also conducting their own investigation into the attacks.

Under the Spotlight

After the final attack, at the Starks farmhouse, authorities and media swarmed into Texarkana like never before. The quiet town was buzzing with news reporters from all across the nation, and reports of the murders were spreading to all areas of the country. Texarkana had never experienced the media's curious eye before.

The famous Texas Rangers stepped into the investigation, headed by the well-known Manuel "Lone Wolf" Gonzaullas. Gonzaullas was the first Ranger captain from Spanish descent, and was known for being a ruthless charmer in his day. He spent a great of his time providing interviews for national newspapers and radio broadcasts about the state of the investigation. He was even found one day taking pictures of the Starks crime scene with a young *Life* magazine reporter; neighbors had reported suspicious lights and sounds from the house when Gonzaullas and the woman were found.

While the local press, headed by the Texarkana Gazette, dubbed the suspected serial killer the "Phantom Killer" or "Phantom Slayer," national media clung to a different name: "The Moonlight Murderer." Because of this title, many believe that the murders were all committed under the full moon, when the nights were in fact at their darkest during the time of the crimes.

A Fruitless Investigation

The entire nation was on the lookout for a masked killer terrorizing young couples, with leads coming in from all areas of the South. In all, the authorities considered over four hundred separate suspects, but no one was ever charged with the attacks of that spring. While most of these suspects never received any public attention, the media caught wind of some of the more notable ones.

A middle-aged man from College Station, a Texas town several miles west of Texarkana, was at one point considered a prime suspect. He had previously been caught sneaking up on parked cars, typically with young couples inside, and brandishing a .22 rifle in order to threaten and rob them. While this man was never convicted of murder, many believed him to be the Phantom Killer based on the similar crime and weapon.

In Fayetteville, a young male graduate student of the University of Arkansas committed suicide. In the wake of his untimely death, a note was found containing a handwritten poem and confession to the murders in Texarkana. His military records showed he had showed "homosexual tendencies" during his time with the U.S. Navy, and at the time these tendencies were believed to be a mental disorder related to sexual crimes like rape or assault. Nothing of value ever came from this lead.

Several local residents accused an IRS agent of the crimes, seemingly because of his antisocial demeanor or because he had gotten on the town's bad side. Another man claimed to have committed the crimes during fits of amnesia. Neither of these claims resulted in an arrest.

In 1999 and 2000, several years after the last murder, an anonymous woman called surviving family members of the Phantom Killer's victims, claiming to be his daughter. She apologized for the actions of his crimes and begged for forgiveness from the families. There is speculation over whether these claims are valid, but many believe them to simply be a cry for attention. After all, the primary suspect of the Phantom Killer murders, Youell Swinney, never had a daughter.

Chasing a Criminal

During his time investigating the Moonlight Murders, Max Tackett, an Arkansas law officer, made a puzzling connection. Before each murder a car had been reported stolen and subsequently abandoned on the side of the rode. This information led police to believe that the Phantom Killer was using stolen vehicles to flee the crime scenes, and then dumping them before disappearing into the night.

The next car reported stolen triggered a police stakeout, with law enforcement hoping to find the killer connected to the vehicle. As police closed in on the stolen vehicle, Peggy Swinney was found to be driving. Police seized the car and took Peggy into custody, where she was questioned on how she came to possess the stolen vehicle.

Peggy revealed that Youell Swinney, a known car thief in Texarkana, had given the car to her, but that wasn't all she had to say. Peggy began telling police how Youell was the Phantom Killer, how he had assaulted and murdered all those couples, and how he had made her promise not to tell anyone. She included details of the crimes that had not been given to the public, information only known by police and the killer himself.

Before the police could move in on Youell Swinney, Peggy's story changed. She claimed that her previous confession was a lie, and that Youell was not the Phantom Killer after all. Eventually law enforcement discovered that Peggy and Youell had recently been married, making her unable to testify against her husband at all. While Youell remained an unofficial suspect, it seemed that the police were unable to touch him. But that changed in 1947, when Youell was arrested for auto theft.

At that time, Youell Swinney already had a long criminal record. He had been previously charged with counterfeiting, burglary, and assault, landing him in the Texas State Penitentiary for many years. After his release, he continued his work as a career criminal, but avoided capture for the time being.

During the investigation, police found evidence that Youell had owned a .32 Colt revolver, the murder weapon used to kill the second and third sets of victims, but that he had recently lost the gun in a failed card game. In hi home was also a shirt with the name "Stark" embroidered on the pocket, but it is unknown whether this shirt was actually connected to the Starks murder in the previous year.

With Youell in custody for auto theft, the police attempted to pin him as Texarkana's Phantom Killer. The man had a history of violence and sexual assault, and the record of stolen cars pointed toward his involvement in the murders. Youell never denied his innocence; he simply stayed quiet and refused to work with the police when questioned. A botched injection of "truth serum" during an interview in Little Rock, Arkansas, would eventually end the authorities' questioning of Youell regarding the Moonlight Murders. He was placed in prison for auto theft.

Youell remained in prison until 1973. Many of his cellmates recounted stories that Youell had told them, ones that included intimate details of the Phantom Killer's murder scenes and heavily suggested that Youell knew more than he let on. In 1994, Youell died a free man, never admitting to the Texarkana murders. To this day, most consider Swinney to be the Phantom Killer, even if he never served time for these crimes.

The Missing Woman

On June 1st, 1948, 21-year-old Virginia Carpenter departed Texarkana by train, on her way to her first semester of studying at the Texas State College for Women. She left Union Station at about 3PM, and headed for Denton, Texas and her new life as an educated woman. On the train ride, she met another student by the name of Marjorie Webster, who she shared a taxi with on the way to their dormitories.

Their taxi driver, Edgar Ray "Jack" Zachary, first dropped off Webster at the Fitzgerald dormitories, and then continued on to Brackenridge Hall, where Carpenter would be staying for the term. Zachary reported seeing Carpenter approach two young men in a yellow convertible outside the dorm, saying that she seemed to recognize them and was excited to see them. The next day, Zachary returned to the dorms to deliver some of Carpenter's luggage that she had forgotten at the station. He placed the trunk at the hall's front entrance and left, but no one ever claimed the luggage. That previous night would be the last time Virginia Carpenter was seen.

On June 4th, Carpenter's boyfriend, Kenny Branham, and her mother reported Virginia missing. After being brushed off by authorities, Mrs. Carpenter and other family members left for Denton late in the evening, hoping to help the police find Virginia.

Within several days, there were airplanes, motorboats, and on-foot search parties scanning the surrounding area for any sign of Virginia. Drivers of yellow convertibles were stopped and questioned, and Zachary was questioned by police and subjected to a polygraph test. Carpenter quickly became one of the most famous missing person cases in Texas, with her picture circulating across the country.

Before long, rumors started spreading back in Texarkana. Virginia Carpenter had personally known three of the Phantom Killer's victims, and some started to believe that she had a target on her back. Perhaps the killer had followed her from Texarkana to Denton, just another passenger on the crowded train. Or perhaps the killer was someone that Carpenter knew, like one of the men seen in the yellow convertible to night she went missing. Either way, many believe that this disappearance was connected to the attacks in 1946.

Countless sightings of Carpenter across Texas - riding in a car, buying groceries, or hitchhiking - continued to flow in, but no solid leads were ever discovered. By 1955, Carpenter was considered dead. She had been missing for seven years, and little hope remained of finding her. Despite this, tips continued to emerge on Carpenter's possible whereabouts.

In 1959, a wooden box was found buried with female remains inside that matched Carpenter's physical description. They were sent to Austin for examination, but the landowners soon confessed to digging them up from an old cemetery.

In 1998, a man called the police claiming to know where Carpenter's body was buried. He led police to the grounds of the Texas State College for Women, the school she was meant to attend, but the search came up empty.

Carpenter's disappearance causes some to doubt Youell Swinney's guilt. If her disappearance was a result of the Phantom Killer, the same man who brutally attacked at least three different couples, then this man could not be Swinney. At the time Carpenter went missing, Swinney was being held in prison for auto theft. Maybe Peggy Swinney had a hand in the disappearance of Carpenter, or her abduction was committed by someone other than the Phantom Killer, but it could not have been Swinney.

Phantoms Around the World

Some believe that the Phantom Killer simply moved his crimes to a new location, but it is likely he just inspired other killers to follow his pattern of attack. As the United States reached the height of violent crime and serial killers, attacks cropped up across the country and even abroad. The Phantom Kiiler's *modus operandi* (or M.O.) would become commonplace among serial killers in the coming decades, including the Zodiac Killer, Il Mostro, and the Son of Sam.

In 1946, a young couple was shot in Fort Lauderdale, Florida. Elaine Eldridge and Lawrence Hogan were parked outside Dania Beach when someone approached the vehicle and shot both victims with a .32 semi-automatic handgun. While the weapon used was not a Colt, it remained very similar to the one used in Texarkana. No fingerprints or footprints were found at the scene. With several similarities to the Texarkana attacks, many believed that the killer had relocated across the country. Texas, Arkansas, and Florida police worked together on the investigation, but no major connections were ever revealed to the public.

Located in San Francisco, the Zodiac Killer operated very similarly to the Phantom Killer during the late 1960s. He stalked young people in their vehicles and shot them with a revolver, and his identity remains unknown. However, unlike the Phantom Killer who personally avoided the media's attention, the Zodiac Killer was hungry for exposure. His main source of fame comes from sending cryptic notes to the Bay Area press, including four ciphers. Only one of these ciphers was ever solved, but it led the police no closer to identifying a suspect. These notes were examined top to bottom, in hopes of finding the true identity of the Zodiac Killer, but no leads were ever found.

Across the Atlantic Ocean, from 1968 to 1985, Florence, Italy was shook by sixteen murders. Dubbed Il Mostro or The Monster of Florence, the killer shot young couples parked alone in their cars with a .22 rifle. While four different suspects were arrested and charged with these murders throughout the years, the investigation has attracted scrutiny and many believe these men were actually innocent.

While the Son of Sam's identity is known today, his killings reflected those of the Phantom Killer and others. Operating in New York City in the mid 1970s, David Berkowitz killed six victims with a .44 Bulldog revolver. His attacks triggered the biggest manhunt in New York City, and for years women kept their hair short and avoided disco clubs for fear of being Berkowitz's next target. Like the Zodiac Killer, Berkowitz loved taunting the police and media with cryptic letters, where he promised to continue killing until he was caught. After his capture in 1977, Berkowitz enjoyed a bit of morbid celebrity for his crimes, which many reported he seemed to enjoy greatly. He remains in prison today, serving six life sentences.

While it is unlikely that the Phantom Killer actually relocated to be the Zodiac Killer or Il Mostro, some true crime experts believe it is possible. While the Phantom Killer was one of the first of his kind, looking back his killings were not exceptionally unique by today's standards.

It is easy to see how the Phantom Killer and his Moonlight Murders have shaped our ideas of killers today. Urban legends of a mad man stalking young couples in love, scratching on car doors and leaving bloody hooks behind, persist around campfires and in dark corners of the Internet. *The Town That Dreaded Sundown* might live among the likes of Freddy Krueger and Michael Myers, but it is a fictionalized retelling of the very real horrors that haunted Texarkana that year.

THE MURDER OF AMY ALLWINE

JESSI DIXON

In May 2016, a team of hackers cracked into a site on the dark web – and unknowingly uncovered evidence that would eventually help investigators with the FBI solve the murder of a woman named Amy Allwine.

"If you want to kill someone, or to beat the shit out of him, we are the right guys," read the homepage of Besa Mafia, a website that was supposedly affiliated with an Albanian organized crime ring. In exchange for bitcoin, they claimed they would arrange beatings and even assassinations. The site had appealed to many potential clients, including a user named "dogdaygod."

The FBI determined that "dogdaygod" was responsible for arranging the murder of Amy Allwine, a church-going Midwestern woman. "Dogdaygod" wanted the slaying to "look like an accident," according to the emails sent to Besa Mafia. The user claimed Amy Allwine "tore my family apart by sleeping with my husband, and is stealing clients from my business."

However, this portrayal of Amy Allwine didn't fit with the victim's life. The 43 year old dog trainer ran her own business in a suburb outside of St. Paul, Minnesota. She'd met her husband, Stephen, at a Christian college, and the couple had continued to pursue their dedication to their faith as active members of a local congregation of the United Church of God. Stephen even served as church elder, providing marriage counselling services to couples who were struggling to stay together. The couple even raised an adopted son.

"Amy was the most motivating person, she was the most positive person," said Jennifer Waters, one of Amy's dog training students. "She had nothing but good things to say about anybody."

Friends and family described Amy as a loving, devoted mother and a compassionate, dedicated friend. She seemed hardly to be the kind of woman "dogdaygod" insisted that she was, but it looked like someone was trying to have her killed.

In July 2016, a woman who called herself Jane sent Amy Allwine the first of two untraceable emails containing threats and insults. Jane said Amy was a "fat bitch" who had destroyed the woman's marriage, and more disturbingly, threatened Amy's family and her son – using details that clearly gave the impression that Jane had the Allwines under surveillance.

"Here is how you can save your family," read Jane's initial email. "Commit suicide."

The email went on to assure Amy that if she did not comply with the sender's instructions to kill herself, she would "slowly see things taken away from you, and each time you will know that you could have stopped it." It also included a list of suggested methods Amy could employ to carry out the grisly deed.

Around the same time, the FBI reached out to the Cottage Grove police department, advising them of the murder-for-hire plot where some unknown user was planning to pay virtual currency to have Amy killed. The police met with the Allwines and recommended they step up their home security. And they did – Stephen even received a permit to carry a handgun on August 10, and purchased a 9mm Springfield XDS to protect his wife.

But just months later, that same gun would be used to kill her.

Murder for hire

The plot to kill Amy appears to have originated on Valentine's Day, according to a timeline later pieced together by investigators from the FBI, Cottage Grove police, and the Minnesota Bureau of Criminal Apprehension. On February 14, 2016, "dogdaygod" attempted to pay $5,000 to have Amy Allwine killed in a car crash.

The user provided Besa Mafia with plenty of information to help them make the murder look like an accident – details of her travel schedule and constant whereabouts. Meanwhile, "dogdaygod" was also searching the dark web for different ways to launder virtual currency like bitcoin to pay for the assassination.

It was the 35-character bitcoin address that police would eventually find on the smartphone of Stephen Allwine – linking Amy's devoted Christian husband to the assassination plot. But the hit man had been unable to follow through with the kill, and police had discovered something else on Stephen's smartphone.

Apparently, the church elder had some dark secrets. Stephen had spent a few months involved in a relationship with a woman he'd met on Ashley Madison – a website specifically for people looking for extramarital affairs. Michelle, Stephen told police, was from the "western metro Twin Cities" area, and investigators were able to locate her.

"She stated that the two had an intimate relationship for several months during which time they took out-of-town trips together, as well as spent time together locally," the police report read. "She admitted their affair was sexual in nature and provided photographs of the two of them together in which they are hugging and kissing."

This wasn't the first woman Stephen Allwine met on Ashley Madison, however. Police also learned that he had gone on a date with another woman in October 2015, whom he met for dinner at a nearby golf course. The evening ended with a kiss, but they never saw each other again.

Michelle, though, maintained an ongoing relationship with Stephen. She recalled instances when Amy was out of town that Stephen had asked her to come to his home, but that she needed to sneak in the back way to avoid being detected by the home security system. The photographs Michelle shared with authorities were from December 2015, and she said the romance "fizzled" by February – around the same time as "dogdaygod" started investigating the possibility of having Amy Allwine killed by an anonymous hit man from Besa Mafia.

Michelle also told police that if the murder-for-hire plot was true, Stephen Allwine was certainly intelligent enough to pull it off.

According to authorities, the murder scene had been staged to look like a suicide – perhaps an attempt to make it look like Amy had given in to the threats that had been emailed to her from the purported woman named Jane. However, investigators determined that Amy Allwine's death was "inconsistent" with suicide, and charged her husband Stephen with the premeditated murder.

"She's probably dead."

It was Stephen who placed the 911 call on November 13, 2016 – informing the dispatcher that he had arrived home with their nine year old son to find his wife dead in their home. Their son had spotted the body first and brought it to Stephen's attention, which is when he called 911.

When police arrived at approximately 7 p.m., pumpkins were roasting in the kitchen – but Stephen and his son were waiting for police in the open garage. He directed officers to the location of his wife's body, in the bedroom. According to the charging document, Amy was lying on the floor with a pool of blood under her head. Although her body was still warm to the touch, the responding officers were unable to detect a pulse. Later, they would state that Amy was "obviously dead."

Lying near Amy's left forearm and elbow was a gun – a 9mm Springfield XDS. According to Amy's parents, she was right handed.

Additionally, police couldn't find any stippling, or powder burns, on her head, indicating that the gun hadn't been against her head when it went off. There was also no gunpowder, soot, or even blood spatter on Amy's hands.

Investigators discovered traces of Amy's blood elsewhere in the house, though, despite evidence that parts of the home had been cleaned recently. Remnants of bloody footprints were uncovered leading back and forth between the kitchen and the bedroom, and detectives determined that it appeared to be evidence of an "attempted cleanup."

"Agents also found nine separate areas of visible transfer stains and bloodlike substance present on the floor between the master bedroom and laundry room, darkest near the bedroom and progressively lighter near the laundry room," the police document read. "These appeared to be bloody footprints, and were only visible when the crime scene team used luminol and not to the naked eye."

Additional footprints were traced throughout the residence – outside the master bedroom, between the couch and kitchen island, between the dining room table and basement door, in the hallway, in the main floor bathroom, and in the child's bedroom. However, the team noted that "the bloody footprints were not found near any access point to the residence except the garage access door."

Despite the numerous security features that had been added to the house since Cottage Grove police had told the Allwines about the virtual threat on Amy's life, there was no evidence that an outside attacker had killed Stephen's wife. He was the only person coming and going from the property, according to footage captured by the security cameras, and authorities found no signs of forced entry.

Just days after the murder, Stephen Allwine was asked specifically about the blood that appeared to have been cleaned up prior to the arrival of the initial responders. He told detectives that he "had no information about this," adding that no one had been previously injured in the home.

According to Stephen, Amy hadn't been feeling well on the day of her death. She'd mentioned being light-headed, but hadn't wanted to see the doctor about it. According to the Allwines' son, who had been at his grandparents' house when Amy was killed, she was feeling dizzy and his father was going to take her to a clinic.

The last time Stephen saw Amy, he told police, was at around 5:30 p.m., when he left to pick up their son to take him to a gym class. Stephen worked in information technology and had two employers, but worked out of a home office in the basement of the family's home

– a regular shift from 6 a.m. until 5 p.m. from Sunday through Wednesday.

On November 13, detectives learned that Stephen had logged in for work at 6:24 a.m., and remained active until 12:13. He took a lunch break of just more than 41 minutes, and at around 2 p.m., called his in-laws to see if they could pick up their son so that he could get more work done. He said he checked on Amy a couple of times throughout the day, and at around 5 p.m., she said she was fine.

At around 5:30, Stephen left the house to pick up the couple's son from Amy's parents' home. He said he intended to bring the child to a gym class that evening, but while filling his vehicle up with gas, he realized he had forgotten his son's gym shorts at home. Instead of going to the gym, he took his son for dinner at Culver's.

Once they arrived back at the house, the child saw his mother's body in the bedroom and asked Stephen why she was sleeping on the floor. Then, he told police, Stephen replied, "she's probably dead," and called 911.

The home security system that the Allwines had installed in the home was set to record the dates and times that the front and garage doors are opened. On November 13, police learned that after Stephen said he left to pick up his son, no one entered or exited the home until Stephen and the child returned.

"Most notably," the police document stated, "the search warrant return also revealed that after (Amy)'s father left the residence at 2:02 p.m., the service door was opened at 2:40 p.m., 2:42 p.m., and 4:40 p.m."

In the statement he made to police, Stephen claimed that once his son had been picked up by his grandfather, he had been working in the basement until he left at 5:26 p.m. But Stephen's employer reported that after his lunch break on November 13, he did not re-enter the phone queue to finish his shift, and didn't enter any case updates that day – "despite the fact that (Stephen) works on customer issues and is supposed to log all of his activity in his case notes."

Stephen's other employer verified that he didn't log in at all on November 13.

Police noted that Stephen's home office contained "a large amount of computer equipment, which appeared to be very sophisticated and technologically advanced" – however, Stephen had denied having any knowledge about hacking or the dark web in his statement. Instead, he said he knows "how things are supposed to work in the legitimate world."

Investigators quickly learned that Stephen had not been truthful with law enforcement regarding his activity on the internet – information gleaned from examining Stephen's computer revealed that he'd been accessing the dark web since as early as 2014.

Absolute determination

After initially reaching out to Besa Mafia on February 15, the user named "dogdaygod" posted on March 6 that "she" needs "this bitch dead." Amy would be traveling to Moline, Illinois, with a companion, on March 19 and 20 – and according to the post "dogdaygod" made on the website, they didn't care if the companion was killed in the hit, as well. Investigators learned that Amy Allwine had indeed traveled to Moline during that time, when she attended a dog training competition.

However, "dogdaygod" was informed on March 20 that the Besa Mafia hitman had not had the opportunity to kill Amy in Moline – leading the user to suggest that Besa Mafia send someone to complete the hit a few weeks later, when Amy would be in Atlanta. Besa Mafia recommended the use of a sniper for an additional ten bitcoin, or approximately $12,000.

"It was ultimately decided between 'dogdaygod' and Besa Mafia that (Amy) would be killed at her home and the house would be burned afterward," stated police documents. "Besa Mafia stated that with the additional ten bitcoin cost, the plan had a 100 per cent success rate. 'Dogdaygod' agreed to provide the money by the next day."

On March 22, "Dogdaygod" attempted to transfer the bitcoin, and provided Besa Mafia with a specific 34-digit alphanumeric address to be matched with the transfer. According to investigators, these bitcoin addresses are considered unique to each transaction – and during a computer forensics search of Stephen's computer, the specific bitcoin address "dogdaygod" had posted was located on a backed up deleted file – "linking (Stephen) directly to 'dogdaygod.'"

Still, though, Besa Mafia's hitman hadn't completed the job. "Dogdaygod" was informed that their hitman had been caught driving a stolen vehicle and had been taken to jail, but according to local police, "no one was apprehended in Minnesota and western Wisconsin and was arrested in a stolen vehicle and in possession of a gun" during this time. But Besa Mafia didn't stop soliciting money from the user, putting off the hit again and again.

"We have zero information at this point that any of the hits that were ordered on that website were actually carried out," a Minnesota detective told Fox 9 news. "In fact, there is pretty good evidence, I think, that it was just a scam."

In May, Besa Mafia was targeted by an ethical hacker, who published the site's customer list and revealed that the entire operation was a scam. The FBI payed close attention and began investigating the site – while "dogdaygod" had to seek out an alternative solution.

The user popped up on another dark web site looking for a drug dealer in the Minneapolis area – and a forensic search of Stephen Allwine's phone revealed cookies from search engines used to search the dark web were installed on his phone at the same time.

The FBI discovered that "dogdaygod" had been trying to access a drug called scopolamine, or "devil's breath." A derivative of nightshade that can be administered as a powder with no discernable flavour or odor, scopolamine is primarily used to treat nausea. However, the drug is also known to erase a person's memory, according to police documents, and "rendering them incapable of exercising their free will."

While investigating the murder of Amy Allwine, police asked the Ramsey County medical examiner's office to test for the presence of scopolamine – and found that the drug was present in her system, at more than 45 times the concentration of a prescription. Amy had never been prescribed the drug.

"It should be noted that a search of (Amy)'s iPhone 6 revealed that on November 13, 2016, it was last used to search 'Vertigo-Wikipedia' at approximately 2:01 p.m.," police documents stated.

Her time of death was estimated by the medical examiner to have been around 3 p.m. – approximately four hours before police were called. Stephen claimed he'd last seen her and spoken to her more than two hours after the estimated time of death, at around 5:30 p.m. He'd gone into the room to tell Amy that he was leaving to pick up their son, and had found her kneeling by the bed.

"(Stephen) stated that he assumed she was praying, which was not unusual," the police report read. "(Stephen) stated before he left, he asked (Amy) how she was feeling, and she stated she was feeling okay."

"A cold and calculating killer."

Within months, police had gathered enough evidence to link Stephen Allwine to the "dogdaygod" account – and alleged that he had killed his wife after Besa Mafia had failed to complete the ordered hit. Prosecutors claimed he'd been motivated by a mix of religious guilt and piety, as divorce was simply not an option for a church elder who regularly provided marriage counselling.

"He was seeing other women, but he didn't want to divorce (Amy) because of his position in the church," the jury was told by Washington County assistant attorney Jamie Lynn Kreuser.

As members of the United Church of God, the Allwines took a conservative stance on marriage and divorce. According to the church's website, marriage is a "commitment for life" where no "recognized troubles" can justify divorcing a mate "with the freedom to remarry."

"Who would want to do this?" asked Kreuser, noting that as a caring mother, dog owner, and woman of faith, Amy Allwine was not the sort of person who would choose to die by suicide. "Someone who didn't want to be married to her anymore."

The incredible lengths Stephen allegedly went to in order to ensure his wife's death also demonstrated a significant level of sophistication, which was noted by Washington County prosecutor Fred A. Fink Jr. He said Stephen's action "appears to be an absolute determination to kill this woman."

Stephen was also the sole benefactor of his wife's $700,000 life insurance policy, prosecutors said.

But the defense argued that there was insufficient physical evidence connecting Stephen with the crime – all forensics had been able to find was a "particle characteristic of gunshot residue" on Stephen's right hand from the sample he'd given to police after Amy's death.

According to Stephen's attorney, Kevin DeVore, prosecutors had built a case on "theories with gaps," and incorporated plenty of speculation to "bridge those gaps."

"It sounds like an amazing story – but it's not a TV show or a movie, but real life," he said. "Just because he had an affair doesn't mean he killed his wife or even didn't love his wife."

The jury disagreed with the defense's argument, despite Fink's own admission that the case was "entirely circumstantial." On January 31, 2018, after just eight hours of deliberation, they found Stephen Allwine guilty of first-degree murder for the premeditated attack on his wife.

Addressing the courtroom at his sentencing just days later, Stephen stated that he had always loved his wife and did not kill her – adding, "I've never asked for anything except to work for God."

"I never went to sleep, and I never woke up without kissing her," he said. "The grief of losing her is tremendous."

He also claimed that the couple had never even argued, noting that "no one ever talked bad about our relationship." During his statement, he insinuated that an unknown assailant had entered the house through a patio door which had been left unlocked.

"Even though she's gone, she's gone knowing I loved her," Stephen said. "The only image I have in my mind is one of my smiling, beautiful wife."

Judge B. William Ekstrum was unable to conceal his irritation, and told Stephen, "you are an incredible actor, a hypocrite, and a cold and calculating killer."

"We're looking at a complete narcissist," Fink added after the sentencing. "His elocution was all about him – not Amy or her death."

"The most complex case."

Ekstrum sentenced Stephen to life in prison with no possibility of parole – the mandatory sentence for a conviction of first degree murder. His term is to be served at St. Cloud Prison. Stephen said that during his time at the Washington County Jail, he's met drug addicts, child molesters, and kidnappers – and had been conducting regular bible study sessions.

"I'm going to take my bible to St. Cloud (Prison)," Stephen said, "and see what happens."

He no longer serves as a church elder, however, as the Council of Elders at the United Church of God removed Stephen from ministry after he was initially charged with Amy's murder in 2017. While the church did release a brief statement following the sentencing, it offered no "speculative comments" regarding the verdict.

"It is our fervent hope that all will continue praying to our merciful Father about the entire situation and be compassionate about what the extended families are going through," the statement read. "We can have confidence that our all-knowing God is aware of all aspects regarding this tragic situation."

Prosecutors were pleased with the result, although Fink noted making the conviction required the jury to almost piece together a "jigsaw puzzle" of evidence.

"We believe the jury did the right thing," he said after the sentence was handed down. "They had a lot of pieces of evidence to go through … I've been doing this 43 years and it's probably the most complex case I've ever tried. It's fair that this defendant spends the rest of his life in prison."

It was also one of the more complex investigations ever undertaken by Cottage Grove police, according to detective Sgt. Randy McAlister. As many as five detectives worked the case over two months – with the first month requiring them to set aside much of the rest of their workload to focus on the investigation full-time.

"I think the big difference between this and a more common murder the dark web, the internet connection – that's what's really been taking a lot of time," he said. "This is the first case involving death threats on a purported dark web website that we've ever dealt with. This is definitely the most in-depth."

Kreuser said that throughout the sensationalized trial, prosecutors stayed focused on the victim and her loved ones – despite significant media attention.

"At the end of the day, justice was served," she said, "and I'm glad for Amy and her family."

Many of Amy's family and friends provided victim impact statements during the six day trial – though few of these accounts were critical of Stephen. The courtroom was filled with people who knew the couple, either through Amy's business or the family's dedication to the church.

"It was very supportive for the entire thing," said DeVore. "It goes beyond the love one might expect."

Still, Amy's parents were stung by Stephen's betrayal, and called him a "selfish person." They added they'd been "astonished" to hear how Stephen had spent months plotting their daughter's murder – at Amy's wedding twenty years earlier, her father remembered how he "put her hand into Steve's and asked him to take good care of my little girl."

Amy's sister, Julie Brown, told the court about how Amy had "lived in fear every waking moment of the last months of her life," thanks to the anonymous death threats she'd received, and the murder-for-hire plot the FBI had warned her about. Even simple tasks like going grocery shopping "spurred intense anxiety" for Amy.

"We've lost so much," Brown said, "but with God's grace, all is not lost."

After the verdict, Amy's parents and siblings released another statement.

"We can summon no words to describe life without Amy," it read. "We loved her and miss her tremendously. We now turn to the path ahead of privately healing and grieving."

THE MURDER OF CARA KNOTT

JESSI DILMONT

Three decades after a murder that shook the city of San Diego to its core, residents and visitors are still reminded of the tragic slaying each time they drive down Interstate 15. Near Mercy Road, where 20 year old San Diego State junior Cara Knott was killed in 1986, hangs a sign that reads "Knott Memorial Bridge."

The killing was difficult enough for the community to swallow – a young, beautiful woman, full of potential, never even lives to see her college graduation. But what made the murder even more horrifying was the arrest that soon followed. California Highway Patrol officer Craig Peyer, who had pulled the student over as she'd been driving home, was charged with killing Cara Knott.

California highways were a dangerous place for women in the decades leading up to Knott's death. Stories of women being abducted, assaulted, or killed at the side of the road were everywhere, and it wasn't unusual for a missing girl to turn up murdered in a California ditch. In 1986, women were afraid of pulling over onto poorly-lit shoulders, alone and vulnerable.

At Peyer's sentencing, Supreme Court Judge Richard Huffman said the officer "took advantage of a position of trust and confidence."

"It terrorized everybody," recalled Paul Pfingst, who'd handled Peyer's retrial in the late 1980s after the first trial resulted in a deadlocked jury. "I have never seen a case that has such a direct impact on people's perception of their safety, especially women. It popped the bubble of perceived safety."

Peyer was found guilty of murder by the jury at the second trial, with the verdict handed down June 22, 1988. In June 2018, 30 years after the jury announced its decision, Knott's mother, Joyce, said she hadn't even been aware of the unfortunate anniversary.

"I think of the dates that have to do with her," she told a reporter with the San Diego Union Tribune, "not that have to do with the trial."

A typical drive home

On December 27, 1986, Cara Knott had been visiting her boyfriend in Escondido. She called her parents shortly after 8 o'clock that evening, letting them know that she'd be on her way back to their El Cajon home shortly. It was a 45 minute drive, and one Knott made quite frequently.

But she never made it back home.

By 10 p.m., when his daughter still hadn't arrived, Sam Knott was overwhelmed by the feeling that she was in danger. He and his wife, Joyce, set out to search for Knott along Interstate 15, the road she usually took between the family's home and her boyfriend's.

As the clock ticked closer to midnight, Sam was becoming increasingly concerned for his daughter's well being. He signalled to a passing highway patrol car and asked the officer to put out an all-points alert for Knott, but was informed that there was nothing the authorities could do until she'd been gone for at least 24 hours. So, Sam and Joyce began their own search – spending the night canvassing the county's freeways and off-ramps, as well as darkened shopping malls and parking lots. But they didn't stop calling the police. During one of Sam's impassioned pleas for help, the dispatcher calmly responded, "girls will be girls."

Knott's sister Cynthia and her brother-in-law Bill Weick, who'd spent the night searching along with Knott's parents, decided at around 5:30 a.m. to venture a little further down an off-ramp at Mercy Road. The road hadn't yet been completed, so it came to an end in a shadowy pit underneath the busy interstate.

"It was foggy and dark and creepy," Weick testified, months later, "like something out of a movie."

As they proceeded slowly past the construction roadblocks, they found Knott's distinctive vehicle. The 1968 Volkswagen Beetle was empty below I-15 at Mercy Road, abandoned near a bridge along the frontage road. The keys were still in the ignition, a credit card was left lying on the driver's seat, and her overnight bag was still sitting in the backseat. Knott, though, had seemingly disappeared.

Panicked, the couple began frantically searching the immediate area – calling Knott's name over and over again before finally reaching out to the police for help. Meanwhile, Sam was speeding down I-15 himself, pursuing a black and white police car with his lights flashing in an attempt to catch the officer's eye. He continued to follow the cruiser as it turned off the freeway onto the Mercy Road exit, and was shocked to see his daughter and his son-in-law waiting near Knott's empty car.

Sam, Cynthia, and Bill were combing the area with police at 8:12 that morning, when Cara Knott's body was found less than a mile away from her car – dumped about 75 feet to the ground below. She'd been strangled before being thrown from the bridge.

"This was one of the most intense investigations I've ever been involved with," said San Diego homicide lieutenant Phil Jarvis, who eventually put three times the typical number of technicians and detectives to work on the case.

What was particularly troubling for Jarvis was Knott's motive. Why had she stopped her car on a cold winter night on an unfinished road that didn't lead anywhere? Time of death had been determined to be sometime between 9 and 10 p.m., and a receipt from a Chevron gas station indicated she'd refuelled at 8:27. The vehicle was working fine, and the passenger-side door was still locked – Cara Knott hadn't been the type to pick up hitchhikers, her family said. There was no sign of a struggle, either.

However, despite the cold weather – one of the coldest nights of the year – her driver-side window was left partly rolled down. To investigators, it seemed like Knott had pulled over for someone she trusted – someone like a police officer.

"Did you choke her?"

The very next day, as the story got out to the news media, a TV reporter contacted California Highway Patrol and asked to interview an officer about what women could do to stay safe while traveling alone at night. She was put in touch with Peyer, who answered her questions, during a ride along on camera, with fresh scratches on his face.

"You never know who you could meet along the road ... Anything could happen," he said to Rory Devine, the reporter with NBC San Diego who went with him on the ride-along. "Being a female, you could be raped, robbed if you're a male, all the way where you could be killed."

It only took a week before the homicide investigative team began looking at Peyer as a potential suspect, despite his clean record and thirteen years with the California Highway Patrol. But evidence linked him to the case – blood and fibers found on Knott's body, and a witness who'd seen Peyer pull Knott over on the evening she was killed.

The scratches on Peyer's face had also aroused suspicion. According to the story Peyer had given, they'd been the result of a fall into a fence lining the parking lot of the California Highway Patrol, but upon further investigation, the fence was determined to be too high up to create the scratches on Peyer's face. Additionally, reports had been collected from witnesses who thought they'd seen Peyer at a gas station around the time of the murder, screaming into the parking lot at high speed and looking troublingly disheveled.

One of the witnesses, an off-duty officer with the San Diego police department, had noticed the scratches on Peyer's face – approximately one hour before Peyer claimed he'd fallen into the fence.

Then, more women came forward with stories of their own, describing Peyer's behaviour when he'd similarly pulled them over, as well. Nearly two dozen calls came in to the department, with the mainly female callers recounting stories of being pulled over by Peyer on that same off-ramp – and, although Peyer hadn't been violent or hostile to any of the women in these cases, he'd certainly left an impression.

While the women claimed Peyer had been relatively friendly, his behaviour had made them feel uncomfortable. Some callers reported that they'd been especially bothered by the way he had gently run his hands along their hair and shoulders. In fact, several complaints had been made about Peyer prior to Knott's murder, but because of Peyer's many years of service and glowing reputation within the department, they'd been simply dismissed.

Then, a witness claimed to have seen a Volkwagen Beetle, assumed to be the car Knott had been driving, accompanied by a marked highway patrol car at the time and place where the murder was thought to have occurred. The last time Knott had been seen alive was only two miles from the place where her body was found, at a Chevron gas station. And the attendant on duty could clearly recall spotting a car marked "California Highway Patrol" pull a U-turn in front of the station just as Knott was driving out of the parking lot.

Peyer's alibi was also determined to be false. His logbook was filled with inaccurate documentation around the time Knott had been killed, and he'd made several changes to traffic tickets he'd issued in the hours after the murder – as noted by the motorists who'd been given the tickets that night. One citation had been handed out with the time of 9:20 written overtop of a scratched out 10:30, issued the night Cara Knott was killed by officer Peyer.

A rope found in Peyer's patrol car was examined by forensic dentist Norman Sperber, who concluded that it appeared to match the marks found around Knott's neck – although later, Sperber would be barred from presenting this evidence in court. A distinctive fiber had been found on Knott's dress, a specific type of gold rayon made by using a yellow pigment rather than a dye, and was the same kind of fabric used on the shoulder patch of Peyer's highway patrol uniform. The microscopic purple fibers found on Knott's body could also be traced back to Peyer.

More specifically, though, a small drop of blood had been discovered on one of the boots Knott had been wearing. The blood type was determined to be AB negative – the rarest type, but consistent with Peyer's. Other genetic markers were also found, but at the time of the investigation, technology was not available for DNA testing to provide conclusive results.

Officers who worked with Peyer testified that he'd begun acting strangely after the murder – frequently requesting updates regarding the status of the investigation, and making repeated attempts to rationalize that the perpetrator's crime was nothing more than a simple mistake. And after an internal investigation at California Highway Patrol was completed, it was revealed that while many of the drivers Peyer had stopped were pulled over for legitimate violations, an overwhelming majority were young women, driving alone – women of a similar age group and physical appearance as Cara Knott.

Peyer's colleagues with the highway patrol knew him as a "hot pencil," who issued up to 250 traffic citations each month. The area around Mercy Road had been a part of his patrol since 1982 – in fact, after the discovery of Knott's body in the area, one of the officers teased, "What happened, Craig, did you choke her for not signing a ticket?"

"Breaking his sacred trust"

Even with the evidence piling up against him, however, it wasn't enough to unanimously convince a jury. The first trial deadlocked with a 7-5 split, with the jury leaning more toward a conviction. So, with another trial looming, the family requested a new prosecutor. And Pfingst, who'd recently moved to San Diego from New York, was up for the challenge.

He told the jury that Peyer's "predatory nature" led him to stop young women driving alone, then order them down the isolated frontage road from the Mercy Road off-ramp – where Knott's body had been found. He posited that, perhaps, Knott and Peyer had engaged in some sort of altercation before Peyer, afraid that the young woman would go to the police, strangled her and threw her from the bridge.

Peyer's darker side was revealed to the court during the course of the trials, as well as in a probation report that had been compiled by the agency following his conviction. According to a probation officer, one of the two women who'd previously been married to Peyer had claimed that after he joined the highway patrol, he started acting like "Mr. Macho," and treated his bad as "a way to flirt."

At the trial, more than 20 young women provided testimony describing how Peyer had pulled them over at night for minor traffic violations – in the same isolated area where Knott's body had been found. According to many of these women, who were eventually allowed to drive away without even a citation, Peyer kept them detained on the desolate off-ramp for an hour and a half or more, asking intrusive questions about their personal lives.

"He just seemed like a lonely guy, bored with his shift," said a woman Peyer had pulled over just a few months before Knott's murder. "He leaned against my car just making chitchat, asking me lots of questions about myself ... I think he liked pulling young women over and being the authority figure. He was a gentleman, but the longer he kept me down there, the more nervous I got."

The jury spent days deliberating the case before finally coming back with a verdict. Knott's mother, Joyce, cried as the foreman announced that Peyer had been found guilty of Knott's murder.

"Words cannot express our emotions," she said. "We attended the trial every day, not out of a sense of duty, but because of our love for Cara."

Cara's father, Samuel Knott, read a prepared statement where he expressed his hope "that this predator will never walk the streets again."

"He kidnapped and murdered our sweet Cara, hiding behind his badge and breaking his sacred trust to society ... We want to make sure this terrible horror does not happen to someone else," he said. "Cara was innocent and she was special."

The case made a significant impact on many who followed it – particularly because of Peyer's previous reputation within the community, and the idea that a trusted member of society could commit such a terrible crime.

"I have been in this business for 44 years, and I have never seen a case affect a community like the Craig Peyer case," said Pfingst. "The only thing that was comparable was Son of Sam, back in New York."

Eventually, Peyer received a sentence of 25 years to life – but he's still never admitted to killing Cara Knott.

It was the second time Superior Court Judge Richard Huffman had presided over an emotional trial for Peyer, and he seemed to have a difficult time remaining composed as he imposed Peyer's sentence. Although he praised the efforts of the California Highway Patrol to restore public faith in the agency after Peyer had been arrested for Knott's murder, he admonished the officials also had to share some of the blame in her death.

He specifically pointed to an incident just one month before Knott was murdered on the dark, private Mercy Road off-ramp, when a mother had called the department with a complaint that Peter had forced her daughter to pull over along the same isolated road. The sergeant who took the complaint failed to take any decisive action to address the incident, Huffman said – "following the bureaucratic pattern of dismissing complaints."

He said officials with the highway patrol let Peyer "continue taking young women to the off-ramp, even after receiving complaints" – and added that the specific sergeant in question had gone so far as to "[commend] Peyer for his tactics."

"The tactics were wrong ... and they led inexorably to this tragedy, sure as the sun came up this morning," Huffman said. He added that if the agency had taken action based on the complaint from this concerned mother instead of dismissing the report, "Cara Knott would be alive and Craig Peyer would not be on his way to state prison."

When he refused a request from the defense to consider the possibility of probation for Peyer, Huffman's voice cracked and he seemed to be holding back tears. According to the judge, he'd received more than 100 letters and petitions on Peyer's behalf, from supporters urging Huffman to be lenient on Peyer, as it was his first offense.

Huffman refused.

"The crime, in this came, was an egregious, brutal crime ... The defendant took advantage of a position of trust and confidence ... He placed himself in a circumstance where he found it necessary to take the life of another person," he said. "... A young woman was brutally murdered on the very threshold of life ... I can't fix anything. All I can do is punish ... There's nothing I can do. One family has almost been destroyed by this, and the sentence that the court will impose will do the same thing to another. There's nothing I can fix."

The Golden Rule

After his daughter's death, Sam Knott put in countless hours establishing the Cara Knott Memorial Oak Garden near where Knott's body was found, in the Los Peñasquitos Canyon Preserve. The garden remains to this day, but is now the San Diego Crime Victims Oak Garden.

Right by the very spot where his daughter took her last breath, Sam Knott passed away in 2000 after suffering a heart attack when leaving the garden.

"I think about Sam a lot," admitted Pfingst. "Sam never recovered from that day ... and, ultimately, it killed him, right where his little girl died."

Peyer was contacted in 2004 by authorities from the District Attorney's Office. They offered to run DNA testing on key evidence as part of a wrongful conviction project, but Peyer declined. He was denied parole shortly after – the board concluded that Peyer continued to show a lack of remorse for the murder, and that although he continued to claim his innocence, he refused to allow anyone to try and prove it.

In 2007, he divorced from his third wife, Karen – whom he'd married just 18 months before Cara Knott's murder. Karen had visited him frequently prior to the termination of the marriage, and had defended her husband's innocence when he was initially convicted and sentenced. As she read the court a prepared four-page statement, she brushed tears off her cheeks. Her statement included references to love, compassion, and religion, and included condolences to the family of Cara Knott, who were seated on the opposite side of the packed courtroom.

"Cara Knott was a gorgeous, vivacious, well-loved young lady. During the trial, I felt the pain her family has had to endure, and I am deeply sorry that she was killed," Karen said. "But my husband was a friendly, vibrant, and well-loved person, too, and in my heart, I know you have the wrong man."

Until that point, Peyer hadn't shown any emotion in the courtroom – he'd even declined the opportunity to testify at this trials, and hadn't provided any public statements about the case at all. But as his wife spoke, he finally broke down in tears.

"From the time of Craig's arrest, he and our entire family have cooperated fully with everyone concerned, with the idea in mind of treating others how you would like to be treated," Karen said.

"Unfortunately, that is not how the world is run; that is not how our legal system is run."

In addition to her bitter words about the legal system, Karen Peyer also expressed disgust with the way the media handled the case. An appeal had been denied to allow defense attorneys to question a reporter from the San Diego Union about documents which had apparently been leaked to the press, including the results of a polygraph test that had been given to Peyer prior to his arrest.

According to Huffman, the California Shield Law protected the reporter from having to provide information about his sources to the court, which frustrated Peyer's attorneys – and his wife.

"Before Craig's arraignment, the media had him tried and convicted," she stated. "By most people's expectations, the first trial was supposed to be a slam-dunk, and, when it wasn't, people began questioning, doubting, wondering. By the start of the second trial, we really believed there could be a fair and impartial trial held here in San Diego."

However, Karen claimed, "rumors" began circulating that things "were not going as planned," and a "tiny little tidbit" was forwarded to the local newspapers.

"A confidential, inadmissible piece of information, a lie detector test ... and now, the media pleads the Shield Act and screams it violates their rights," Karen said. "But it was all right for them to violate Craig's rights to a fair trial and to be above the law."

Her statement concluded with an expression of love toward her husband.

"I love you Craig, and I am glad to be your wife," she said. "I will always be committed to you."

Peyer's elderly parents also visited him in prison regularly, every other month, but both passed away in 2010.

A second parole request in 2008 was denied, and a third bid was rejected in 2012. At that time, the board ruled that Peyer wouldn't be eligible again for another 15 years – the longest time permitted under California state law. In 2027, when Peyer will once again be up for parole, he will be 77 years old.

Each time, Joyce Knott traveled to the prison to plead her case – to persuade the board not to grant parole to this man she now refers to as "the monster."

"I dread it. It's a dreadful thing to have to do," she said. "It's kind of beyond anything you can imagine, to go up and go into prison and go through those doors, and to be taken to this room and then the monster comes in."

The board of parole hearings also reads submitted letters, and Joyce always fiercely encouraged the public to send in a letter on her daughter's behalf, requesting that Peyer continue to be held behind bars. Obviously, her advocacy paid off.

Now in his late 60s, Peyer is serving his time at the California Men's Colony, a state prison located in San Luis Obispo. In 2008, at his second parole hearing, he told the board he had a "nearly unblemished prison record," and that he had "worked as an electrician at the facility" for several years – earning himself a salary of $52 per month in 2003.

"She's always with us."

Cara Knott would be in her 50s – and her mother, Joyce, said she still thinks about her daughter every day.

The third of Joyce and Sam's four children, Knott was "tender-hearted," Joyce recalled. An artist, an animal lover, and someone who "always had time for everybody."

"Her big thing was to be a mother and she really wanted to have children," Joyce said. "I have four grandchildren. I should have more, but I won't."

For more than a decade, Joyce was unable to touch the room her daughter had left vacant. But about fifteen years ago, it was time to put away some of Knott's old things and redo the empty bedroom – "which takes some courage," she admitted. When she pulled off the old wallpaper, though, Joyce uncovered a heartwarming surprise: carefully drawn flowers, with handwritten words left by her daughter – "My name is Cara Evelyn Knott. I am 14 years old."

"I appreciate the fact that people remember (her)," Joyce said. "She's always with us."

Knott's murder has had a lasting impact, however – in addition to inspiring several books and episodes of television shows like Forensic Files and Investigation Discovery's Unusual Suspects, the case led to a change in state legislation.

Following the crime and the subsequent trial, many solo female drivers began refusing to pull over when ordered to do so by police officers or highway patrol. In response, the State of California issued a new mandate, allowing that drivers traveling alone would be able to proceed to a high-profile area if ordered to stop – a location like a mall or a gas station, with an increased likelihood of witnesses.

THE COLD CASE OF LEAH ROBERTS

CHELSEA CROSS

When a loved one goes missing, the people closest to them who find themselves left behind often become consumed with the task of finding them. It is a relief to discover them, alive or dead, because then the mystery is solved, at least in part. However, when a person disappears and has yet to be found, what remains in place of them are the unanswered questions, worries, and strong emotions such as rage, guilt, sorrow, or unfathomable loneliness. The case of Leah Robert's is but one example of a missing person's case turned cold, with no new leads despite national attention and multiple re-dramatizations on shows like Unsolved Mysteries and Investigation Discovery. Her older sister and brother, Kara and Heath Roberts, are still searching for her although nearly seventeen years have gone by since her disappearance. Hopefully, someday soon, they will find answers.

Leah's white 1993 Jeep Cherokee had been found on March 18th, 2000. Some sources state that the vehicle was an SUV, which is a common contradiction in this case. Depending on which source you read can even affect how you feel about Leah as a person. With many unanswered questions, people have a natural tendency to fill in the blanks themselves. There were many clues in and around the Leah's vehicle, where her personal affects had been scattered about and left behind, but there was no sign of Leah. There are just as many unknowns as there are hints about what happened to her and where she could be. Among all the other mysterious circumstances surrounding her disappearance, there are hints of Jack Kerouac's influence. Kerouac, who was a Beat Generation novelist, is best known for *On the Road*, although Leah was also a big fan of another work of his known as *The Dharma Bums*. The latter novel depicts scenes of the area where her jeep was found and the former novel described a life of freedom from constraints, which begs the question: how closely might Leah have been trying to follow Kerouac's lead? Or was her presence in the area the product of something more sinister?

Her brother and sister might spend the rest of their lives looking for closure in their sister's disappearance. There is still a reward of $10,000 being offered for further information. Her siblings and the organization they have partnered with, Community United Effort, believe that even the coldest cases can be solved. It is important to remember that the answers might be difficult to hear: was Leah Roberts a victim of a kidnapping or murder? Was she mentally ill and simply lost herself in the expanses of a Washington forest or had she intentionally committed suicide? The evidence in her jeep, at least, tells us that she was not killed in the wreckage of her car, and so perhaps she managed to escaped a total of two car crashes during her life. However, by the time that her jeep had rolled several times over down a steep hill and into the forest, Leah Roberts may have already been dead. It is impossible to know for sure without someone coming forward with more details.

Early Life

Leah Toby Roberts had blue eyes and sandy blonde hair. She did not have an easy life. Although her childhood seemed normal for that part of Durham, North Carolina: a loving family with two siblings, Heath and Kara, for her to squabble and play together. Her grade school life also seemed average, and she obtained good enough grades to get accepted into North Carolina State University, which is when the first of the many tragedies in their lives struck: her family learned that her father had a serious, chronic lung illness. She was seventeen at the time, and despite the dark news, she was able to maintain her grades and stay in school that year. When she was twenty and working at completing her sophomore year at university, the second family tragedy struck: heart disease claimed her mother's life unexpectedly. In order to grieve and adjust to life after her mother, Leah took some time off of school. Shortly after returning to school in 1998, Leah was in a horrific car accident, in which her lung was punctured and her femur was shattered. She had an identifying surgical scar on her hip where a metal rod had been inserted in order to help the bone growth of her femur. When she awoke in the hospital, she claimed that she had gained a new lease on life. In order to recover, she again left school for a short time.

After these three bleak events shook up her life, Leah managed to press on with a new verve. She continued her education in Spanish and Anthropology, and was set to go to Costa Rica for a field program in order to obtain higher fluency in Spanish. It was at that time that the final tragedy in her early twenties occurred. Her father died mere weeks before she was set to leave the country. However, she doggedly continued to prepare and leave for her trip, while leaving her mourning siblings behind to care for the estate. After the field program concluded, Leah spent a little longer in school before deciding that she would discontinue her program just before beginning her final semester. Both of her siblings urged her to stay in school for the final six months, but she could not be persuaded. Heath told reporters that he thought "that all of those things together had the cumulative effect of making Leah even more introspective and probably more aware that, although she didn't know what she wanted to do, I think she was unhappy that she wasn't achieving it." Her sister Kara, on the *Larry King Live* show, said to the audience and viewers that by "the time Leah was 22 she had lost both of her parents and here she is on the verge of graduating from college and I think she just felt lost and didn't have a lot of direction, and I feel like this took this trip as a soul-searching trip." A friend of hers named Susie Smith reported that "Leah is just a very awesome person. Everybody that meets her likes her. Very personable, great smile. But, you know, she was kind of private also. Definitely." These three comments paint a picture of an intelligent, insightful, and kindhearted young woman who was experiencing deep agony. Instead of staying in school, Leah seemed to completely turn her life direction around. She decided to pick up photography and guitar, adopting a kitten, and writing poetry in local coffeehouses. Somewhere in this time,

Leah began to discuss her fondness for the novelist Jack Kerouac.

Road Trip and Disappearance

Shortly after she began to frequent the local coffee shop with her poetry, she made new friends such as Jeannine Quiller and her roommate, Nicole Bennett. Leah often discussed taking a trip like the ones detailed in Kerouac's novels with the other young women. Jeannine has said that "from the last conversation that we had, we were talking about *Dharma Bums* and about how Kerouac was up on Desolation Peak, just taking in all the beauty around him." This was the dream trip that her sister Kara now suspects was Leah's attempt to soul-search as she tried to recover from the five year span of shocking events and sudden losses. During her stints at the coffee shop, she wrote a lot of poetry, and she spent much of her time there reflecting on the meaning of life. Finally, in March, Leah and Kara had spoken to each other on the phone about what they were hopeful about in the coming year. Throughout this conversation, Kara felt that things looked like they were coming around for Leah. Kara recollects that the two sisters had committed to seeing each other in the coming week when the phone call ended.

Around the same time as that phone call, on March 9th, Leah and Nicole applied for a babysitting gig they would need to be at the following day. After that, Nicole left for work, and by the time she returned home, Leah's jeep was gone. Without school or a job, Leah's schedule had been sporadic, so Nicole did not become suspicious until Leah missed the babysitting shift the next day. Leah went unheard from on March 11th, again on March 12th, until finally, she was reported missing to the Durham police on March 13th by Kara.

Kara and Nicole went through Leah's belongings on March 14th in order to find some hints about where she might be. They found a note left by Leah that said: "I'm not suicidal. I'm the opposite. Remember Jack Kerouac." To end the note, Leah had drawn a Cheshire Cat's grin, which hadn't garnered any sort of significance in the press, even now. The other unusual part of the note is that Leah had left it in her room in plain sight, but not on the kitchen counter or on the fridge. For some reason, Leah had assumed that someone would be going into her room or through her possessions. This is also where she left her portion of the rent for the upcoming month. Among the missing was Leah's kitten, although no one knew for sure whether or not Leah had taken her along until later. During her trip to Costa Rica, Leah had given Kara the power of attorney over her bank accounts, which Kara also used to try and determine what was going on with her sister. There were gas station entries as well as motel rooms and other small purchases and larger cash withdrawals, which traced a trail to the northwest.

However, after the card was used to buy gas on the 13th, the usage of the card stopped. Despite no new purchases, at that time no one had any reason to suspect that Leah had met with foul play. Once Kara came into contact with Leah's friend Jeannine and spoken to her about their mutual love for Kerouac, Kara felt reassured that she knew Leah's plan and went back to her own day to day life. However, on March 18th, Kara expected a Happy Birthday phone call from Leah, but never received it. Instead, on that day, she received a letter from the Durham County sheriff's office in her door's mailbox with instructions to call the Whatcom County Sheriff's office in Bellingham, Washington. Upon making that call, Kara was suddenly faced with the fifth tragedy in her young life. After her father's diagnosis, her mother's death, Leah's car accident, her father's death, Kara now had to deal with Leah's disappearance and potential death or suicide.

The car was discovered by two joggers who came upon several articles of clothing tied in trees, although some sources allege that the clothing was merely hanging off of the tree branches. They then followed the scattered clothing along a trail down a treacherous embankment to a white jeep, which was in poor condition. It was off the side of a small road named Canyon Creek Road, which connected to the Mount Baker Highway, which leads to some residences and logging camps at the base and throughout the Mount Baker-Snoqualmie National Forest, which is located a small ways south of the US-Canadian border. Leah was not there when the jeep was discovered, the jogging couple had not seen any signs of her in the area besides the strangely placed articles of clothing. Kara and Heath flew out to meet investigators in Bellingham in order to aid with the search and further investigation.

The Investigation

The jeep had been traveling approximately 40 miles an hour when it left Canyon Creek Road and crashed into the forest. Investigators were able to determine the speed of the vehicle by examining the damage done to it and the nearby vegetation. The insides of the jeep had clothing and pillows set up and placed about as if the vehicle had been used as some sort of shelter, however, the other contents were thrown around and jumbled up, which are traits of a multiple rollover event. Kevin McFadden of the Whatcom County Sheriff's Office said that the driver should have been injured: "With the speed that the vehicle was traveling and the amount of damage to the vehicle, you would anticipate some type of injury to the person inside. At least some type of evidence to indicate contact damage, that the person had been inside the vehicle ... we brought in dogs, we brought in search and rescue, and did a complete grid search up and down the road. But they weren't able to find any indication that anybody had left that vehicle." For some reason, someone had placed the pillows and clothing to form a shelter, but did not pickup the scattered belongings of Leah, some of which included quite a bit of cash ($2,500) and jewelery. Her guitar and cds were also untouched. A small cat carrier and some food were also on the sign, which indicated that Leah had brought her kitten with her. Like Leah, Bea the kitten has never been found. An important clue was found in her belongings as well, which helped investigators understand when she arrived in the area, and that was an innocuous ticket stub for the movie American Beauty on March 13th, which aired at the Bellis Fair shopping mall. That meant that Leah had purchased gas in Oregon and then spent a few hours in the town after the 5-6 hour drive. Besides the fact that her belongings were spread-out everywhere around the crash site, there were none of the signs of the blunt force trauma that normally come standard in a multiple rollover style car crash such as fractured glass or blood, however. Since then, there has been evidence found of the starter being tampered with, which lends itself to the suggestion that the vehicle was empty when the accident occurred.

After Kara and Heath arrived, they began to ask questions in the neighboring town of Bellingham and passed out papers with Leah's picture and information on them. They spoke to businesses where Leah might have gone, although the amount of cash found in her jeans pointed to her buying very little in the town. They headed to the only sit-down restaurant that the Bellis Fair Mall offered, because Kara had an instinct that Leah may have eaten there before or after seeing the movie. The restaurant management led the officers to two men, one of whom claimed that Leah had left the establishment with a man named Barry and created a sketching of him for the police. None of the other patrons or the other man could verify whether or not Leah had actually left with someone, but police did note that on the security footage obtained from that gas station in Oregon, Leah kept searching the parking lot as if someone had been waiting for her. Unfortunately, the gas station had not had security cameras monitoring their parking lot, although officers do believe that there was no one else in the car with her.

One of the biggest indicators to police that Leah had met with foul play was the engagement ring that they had found under the car mat in her car. The ring belonged to Leah's mother, and she never went without it, as it served a constant reminder of her mother. Her roommate Nicole Bennett also knows about the ring: "As long as I've known Leah, she has worn her mother's engagement ring. It was her most prized possession. And when we discovered that the ring had been found in the car, it was definitely, for me, a bad sign." Those close to Leah have gone on record as saying that she wouldn't have taken it off unless she felt she had to, or if she was completely unaware. Some have suggested that Leah may have been in a fugue state, which is officially known as Dissociative fugue and is classed as a DSM-5 Dissociative Disorder. Normally fugue shapes are temporary and last from a few hours to to days, but there are rare instances in which they can last for months. These fugue states are often accompanied with sudden travel and establishing a new identity. There is a lot of parallel between the DSM-5 definition and Leah's case, with a few small differences including the fact that Leah had planned the trip somewhat substantially. Although in Oregon she was considered to be in good shape, a man had called in a panicked sighting of Leah in Everett, Washington, which is likely when she was last seen.

What We Know Now

Since the day of the accident, the widespread area where Leah disappeared has been subject to repeat searches by cadaver dogs and metal detectors, looking for the metal rod that Leah had had put in when her femur had shattered. The *Unsolved Mystery* show aired a segment on her disappearance back in 2001, when its segment still played on Lifetime. None of the tips that came as a result of the broadcast led the investigators to anything worthwhile. Kara teamed up with Monica Caison, who is an expert in solving cold cases by drawing consistent media and national attention to them. On a now annual basis, Kara and Caison organize a caravan through Caison's organization, Community United Effort, which travels the route Leah had likely taken during her fateful trip. They both went onto the Larry King Live, and Kara told the viewers: "I don't really know how I would have made it through the past five years without [Caison] ... We're just trying to, you know, keep Leah's face out there as much as possible."

Near the time of the Investigation Discovery airing of Leah's case in 2011, two investigators had been handed the care of Leah's vehicle, which Kara had asked the police station to protect. They found new evidence that had been ignored in the original investigation. There was a male's DNA on Leah's clothing, and they were the investigators who noticed that the starter relay in the jeep had been altered. The alteration made it clear that Leah did not have to be in the car, nor no one had to be, in order for the vehicle to continue acceleration until its demise. The investigators noted that the man who had originally told investigator about the mysterious third man, named "Barry", had been a mechanic and ex-military. They began to suspect him, and they made actions to get his DNA and fingerprints examined, but he had moved to Canada in the years since the initial investigation, which made the process more difficult. By the time the *Disappearance* episode on Investigation Discovery had aired, the fingerprints had come back negative and the DNA had yet to be processed. He has allegedly commented on online forums protesting his innocence.

Kerouac's Influence on Modern Youth

Jack Kerouac's writing and lifestyle have had an obvious influence on Leah and her missing persons case. He is known as an author of the Beat Generation, and he is likely the most famous. Although his writings were largely anti-capitalistic, very quickly his novels became very popular, and the bohemian lifestyle depicted within morphed into a Hollywood-style spectacle. Years later, however, these ideas of Kerouac returned to the youth they were originally meant for, and inspired Leah to take her road trip. Even during the height of Kerouac's popularity, his ideals were heavily criticized and served as scapegoats for many of the political problems of the age. It seemed as though the thoughts expressed within *On the Road* were offending everyone who wasn't a beatnik. That said, he influenced Bob Dylan's political flare as well as newer writers and philosophers like Sven Birkerts and Thomas Pynchon. Students all over the country were reading him in the 60s and 70s, despite *On the Road* not being added to the curriculum until much later. The novel addresses the dissatisfaction with mainstream culture that some factions of America possess, and has remained as part of the cultural background ever since. Multiple editions have been published since the original, each honoring some facet of the novel—the original manuscript, for example, or a marked anniversary.

Into the 21st century, the book remains a heavy influence of counter-cultures such as hipster, dust punk, and the bohemian lifestyle, which brings us back to Leah Roberts. On the Road, among Kerouac's other works, remains a steadfast influence on the youth of today who are unable to cope with the pressures of modern American society. Although Leah was seemingly a part of the mainstream that counter-cultures reject, the sudden loss and traumas that she had experienced in such a short time span might have parallels with the pressure to achieve. Leah was maintaining her grades throughout adverse circumstances, and there is no way of telling how much pressure she was applying to herself, but the sudden decision to drop out of university so close to it being finished acknowledges that she was under considerable stress. The freedom from stressors that life on the road offered must have been very tempting for her.

Conclusion

Mysteries and missing persons' cases are equal parts thrilling and chilling because they could happen to anyone. In 2012 alone there was upwards of 700,000 missing persons cases in the United States and at any one time there are approximately 90,000 persons missing on average. Of those 90,000, two thirds are adults, and there is a relatively even gender split. About half are white, which includes Hispanic ancestry. Unlike Leah Roberts' case, however, most missing persons in the United States are found. Although the first day or two are the most integral, and it may be that Leah's case had been reported too late. It is actually rare for someone to disappear without a trace, which makes Leah's case all the more unusual and frightening. Perhaps if she had kept a more regular schedule, her friends and family may have been more concerned about her road trip. Her face remains a national news icon, and her sister and brother are still actively searching for her, even if her file has gone cold. It is hard to answer why she hasn't been found yet, and there are still too many unsolved riddles regarding her disappearance.

Leah had many reasons to be depressed or mentally ill, but so did her sister and brother. It is likely that she did not commit suicide, but the possibility is still there. Why did she suddenly drop out of university? Up until then, she seemed to be a highly motivated individual, despite having to miss a few semesters of school due to personal tragedies. The investigators have gone on record saying that "you can't rule out foul play when you don't see somebody for over a year, but there's no evidence to indicate that that has happened. We did process the vehicle for your typical evidence, hairs and fibers and blood, but there was nothing to indicate that happened." Could Leah have been kidnapped or murdered a long ways away from her vehicle and the crash site? Many online commenters suggest that perhaps Leah made herself a new person and has kept out of the national spotlight, despite how difficult that would be in the modern age and considering that her attempt to disappear would have been most likely caused by a fugue state. Some have suggested that Leah wanted to live as free as Kerouac did within his novels, although her sister Kara doubts that theory: "I can understand Leah's needing to get away and find some peace within herself, but considering the loss that our family's experienced, it's difficult for me to think that she would leave us open for another loss like this." Likely, Leah wanted a Kerouac-inspired vacation from her society and instead she met with yet another horrible tragedy.

SPREE KILLER: THE TRUE STORY OF AMY BISHOP

ANNA MASON

Amy Bishop Biography

When you think about school shootings, the first thing that will come to mind is troubled students going on a killing spree and murdering their peers without any good reason. Even though similar crimes happened numerous times in the past, the thorough coverage of Columbine turned school shootings into worldwide news. The experts started to recognize it as a real problem because the frequency increased after 1999 even though the security at schools and universities improved greatly. But what happens when a renowned professor snaps, pulls out their gun, and start killing their colleagues?

This is exactly what happened in University of Alabama in Huntsville back in February of 2010. Amy Bishop, a biology professor who seemed perfectly fine on the outside decided to attack the faculty members at a routine department meeting. Her violent and criminal past emerged after the event, sparking a debate whether this school shooting could have been prevented if the authorities acted sooner and recognized the signs of psychological problems she had since her twenties.

The shooting at the University of Alabama in Huntsville shocked the nation and the fact that the professor was the perpetrator proved that absolutely anyone can suffer a breakdown. Of course, there were countless problems that Amy Bishop had with her friends and co-workers at the university prior to this crime. But there were also some questionable details in her past which made the public certain that this wasn't her first murder.

Early life and education

Amy Bishop was born on April 24th in 1965 in Massachusetts. It was obvious from her early age that she was incredibly clever and gifted child. Amy loved science and wanted nothing more than to expand her knowledge and reach academic success. Her parents were highly educated and wanted to provide Amy with all possibilities to pursue her education. As a matter of fact, her father was an art professor at the well-known Northeastern University in Massachusetts.

Amy did end up enrolling into that same university and earned her bachelor's degree there. Of course, she wanted to go even further and accepted a challenge eagerly. She completed her Ph.D. at the Harvard University shortly after and her field of study was genetics. The very fact that her thesis was incredibly long and well researched will tell you a lot about her character and personality. Amy wasn't a quitter and had the need to be at the top of her class no matter what.

In the midst of her pursuit for knowledge, she managed to start a family and married James Anderson. Even though they had a turbulent relationship at first, they somehow made it work. The two of them have four children together. Amy's life seemed completely normal from the outside – she has a large and loving family, was interested in literature, and worked as a professor at a famous university. However, she wasn't a stranger to odd behavior and was often involved in unexplainable circumstances that did put her on the police's radar.

The first brush with the law

The first questionable event happened on the 8th of December 1986 when Amy was only 21 years old. She accidentally killed her younger brother with a shotgun. The whole accident does seem a bit strange right now but the inquiry into the shooting came to the conclusion that Amy didn't want to murder her brother and that the shotgun somehow misfired.

Apparently, the incident happened in the kitchen of the Bishop family house and Amy discharged the shotgun into her brother's chest. Their mother witnessed the entire event because she was in the same room and testified on Amy's behalf. On the other hand, the authorities did discover that Amy fired one shot into her bedroom wall prior to killing her brother. They did take a very close look at every single detail of this case but concluded that there was no intention behind this murder.

Amy was cleared of any suspicion but the event did not sit well with some of the officers working in Braintree at that time. The statements and files regarding the murder did disappear in 1988 but they were uncovered in 2010 leading to a brand new investigation even though the murder itself happened back in the 1980s. A couple of policemen that took on the case did come out publicly to say that the Braintree law enforcement was heavily corrupted back then and that Amy's mother had connections to people in charge. She insisted on meeting with the police chief at the time and Amy was set free a couple of hours later.

It is important to mention that Amy was in a relationship with her future husband back at the time of the murder but they were on a break. James returned to Amy shortly after and they rekindled their romance. He stood by her and believed in her innocence. The couple was soon married and moved on.

The accounts of the incident do vary and it is unknown why Amy shot her brother in the first place. It seems like it wasn't an accident due to the fact that a total of two shots were fired that night. Neighbors living near the Bishops did think that the brother and sister were arguing earlier that day but they couldn't provide the police with more details. It was later discovered that Amy fled the scene after shooting her brother and threatened two car dealership clerks with the same shotgun in order to attain a car, possibly to run away from the authorities. Amy did not suffer any consequences and continued to live her life as before but this crime will catch up with her.

The bomb in a letter

Amy Bishop's life continued to be hectic in the 1990s as well. But this time she had an accomplice – her husband. Paul Rosenberg worked with Bishop at the Children's Hospital at Boston and was her supervisor. In 1993 he received a package in the mail containing two homemade pipe bombs that didn't go off after he opened it. They were either broken or weren't assembled properly. Rosenberg called the police and they shortly narrowed down the list of suspects.

Amy Bishop loved her job at the Children's Hospital and was very concerned about the negative report she received from Paul Rosenberg. She was forced to resign from her position due to the fact that Rosenberg thought she wasn't a good fit for the hospital and that she lacked experience. After receiving her evaluation, Amy was visibly upset and showed signs of a possible mental breakdown in front of her co-workers.

Amy's psychological state had a huge influence on her husband as well and he was sure that Paul Rosenberg's evaluation was faulty. He became angry with Amy's supervisor and one witness who contacted the law enforcement once the investigation started said that James Anderson wanted to murder Paul Rosenberg because he fired his wife.

The police didn't have any solid evidence that could connect Amy Bishop and James Anderson directly to the pipe bombs. The spouses refused to let the detectives search their home in order to find any traces of explosives and they stopped talking and communicating with them as well.

The investigators were sure that Bishop and Anderson made the bombs but the lack of evidence left the murder attempt unsolved. This case will be revisited after the shooting at the University of Alabama but the investigators would not reach a definite conclusion. The judge confirmed that she was certain Amy Bishop and her husband were the ones who sent the package to Paul Rosenberg even though there were no physical traces anywhere on the bombs or package. They were the only ones who wanted to harm the doctor and had strong negative feelings toward him.

Anger management issues

The next incident that involved Amy Bishop happened in an International House of Pancakes. Even though it seems trivial, the attack was an evidence that Amy had a lot of unresolved psychological issues that were starting to come out to the surface. The inability to get the last booster seat led to a sudden burst of aggression towards another guest of the restaurant.

Bishop casually strolled to this woman's table and asked her to give her the booster seat. When the woman refused, Bishop swung her arm and hit the woman in her face screaming at the top of her lungs: "I am Dr. Amy Bishop!" The other guests who witnessed the incident were shocked by Bishop's behavior and called the authorities right away.

Amy Bishop ended up in the police station, accepting the full responsibility for the attack without showing any remorse for her violent behavior. She pleaded guilty and received probation. The attorneys who prosecuted her demanded that Bishop attends anger management classes but it seems like the judge ignored their demands. There were no records that Bishop ever attended any or received psychological help in order to deal with her issues.

Career at the University of Alabama

Amy Bishop and her husband continued to be heavily involved in the scientific community and they worked together on several projects. They invented the portable cell incubator which won a couple of awards and they moved on to perfecting their invention with some financial help from people interested in using their incubator in the near future.

Amy Bishop worked at Harvard Medical School before she relocated to the University of Alabama in Huntsville back in 2003. She applied for a position of an assistant teacher and got accepted. Her academic achievements spoke for themselves and the university though she would be a valuable addition to their biology department.

Other professors who worked closely with Bishop did testify that she was slightly strange and would often speak about topics unrelated to a discussion they were having at the moment. But it wasn't alarming at all. It fit her character because she was known to be slightly odd. Bishop didn't manage to fit in and she wasn't a favorite among students either. They would often complain that Bishop wasn't a good professor and was unable to share her knowledge with the rest of the class properly. It was clear that she was smart but Amy simply wasn't made to be a lecturer and it showed.

She lacked charisma, patience, communication skills, and the students would often leave her lectures completely confused. Science teachers often get very involved in their studies which might lead them to become antisocial and withdrawn from the rest of the society. Bishop could be very unpleasant to a class she was teaching and numerous students left the university because of her. The complaints continued to be filed for years but they didn't have any effect.

After six years at the University of Alabama, Amy Bishop was once again under review and the committee decided that they will terminate her contract, making the 2010 spring semester her last one at that institution. She tried to file a complaint to the tenure but the chances are she would be leaving the university very soon.

As you might have guessed, the news shocked Bishop and she probably started spinning out of control from the very moment she was told that they were letting her go. We could blame the tenure for this incident but it simply isn't enough. Bishop's personality that rarely accepted failure combined with the underlying aggression she carried inside made this seemingly normal woman to snap. After all, the position of a professor was something she worked her whole life for and there was no way she would go away so easily.

Amy managed to find out what led to the negative review and discovered that her colleagues were partly to blame. They told the committee that she was odd and slightly crazy, citing all the student complaints that kept piling in over the years. She decided to hit them back and contacted Equal Employment Opportunity Commission saying that her colleagues were discriminating her because of her gender. She was certain that the fact that she was a woman was the core of the problem. Bishop's colleagues stood by their statements and

Equal Employment Opportunity Commission couldn't find anything that would prove Bishop's claims of gender discrimination.

Amy Bishop's contract was supposed to end on 12th February but she would continue teaching at the university for a few more weeks. It was apparent that Amy's mental health was falling apart but her husband still stood by his wife's side and supported her fight to stay at this institution. February 12th, 2010 marks the date when the situation at the University of Alabama escalated and Amy Bishop opened fire on her colleagues at a routine faculty members meeting.

She waited patiently for her opportunity and there was no way she could allow the moment to get away for her. The date carries a lot of symbolism to her and it seems like she saw it as her personal vendetta against the other professors working at the same department. She felt betrayed by the team she closely collaborated with for years and the only way she could get her way was by murdering every single one of them.

The day of the shooting

On the 12th of February, everything was going smoothly at the university. Classes were being held and students attended lectures – there were no signs that anything could go wrong. Amy Bishop followed her schedule for the day as well, teaching two classes in the morning and around the noon. The students who were in her anatomy and neuroscience classes would later say that they didn't notice any changes in Bishop's behavior.

A standard faculty meeting was planned to start later in the afternoon. The professors working at the Biology and Mathematics departments slowly gathered in the Room 369 and occupied their seats. Everyone was there including Bishop. She listened to everything that was discussed at the meeting but kept to herself without speaking too much unless asked to do so. There were thirteen faculty members in the room.

Amy Bishop stood up in the middle of the meeting and pulled out a 9mm handgun. It would be later discovered that she didn't have a valid permission to carry any firearm with her. She apparently took the gun from her husband without his knowledge. Joseph Ng who worked as a fellow professor at the University of Alabama at Huntsville would later state: "Bishop got up suddenly, took out a gun and started shooting at each one of us. She started with the one closest to her, and went down the row shooting her targets in the head." Other witness described the killings as "execution style". It was clear that Bishop knew what she was doing and who she wanted dead.

But the unexpected thing happened right in the middle of the attack – her handgun either run out of bullets or got jammed. Bishop was pulling the trigger but the gun would only click. This prevented a larger catastrophe. This setback agitated Bishop and it was the perfect time for Joseph Ng to step in and try to keep her from attacking the rest of the faculty members. He carefully got closer to Bishop and other professors joined him. They managed to push Bishop through the door. She ended up in the hallway while her colleagues stayed in the meeting room. They started barricading themselves inside and called the local police.

Amy Bishop was arrested shortly after the shooting. Sheriff's deputy was one of the first responders and he approached her with confidence even though she could have been armed. The law enforcement found her standing in front of the Shelby Center for Science and Technology and she didn't try to run away or resist the arrest. As a matter of fact, she seemed to be completely unaware of the events that happened in the Room 369. The arresting police officers asked her why she killed her colleagues and she responded by saying that she didn't hurt anyone and that the faculty members were alive and well.

The law enforcement entered the building alongside the emergency personnel. They tended the wounded professors and took a closer look at the crime scene. The pistol which was used in the shooting was discovered in the bathroom. Amy Bishop probably placed it there before exiting the building in an attempt to distance herself from the weapon.

In the end, Amy Bishop murdered three of her colleagues and wounded three more. Gopi Podila was the head of the biology department and Bishop probably held a grudge against him the most. Maria Ragland Davis and Adriel D. Johnson Sr. were fellow biology professors working at the University of Alabama for years. It is a huge tragedy that could have been prevented if the authorities did their job properly decades ago. The fact that the gun stopped working in the middle of the killing spree probably saved many lives. It is important to mention that only a handful of students were actually in the building during the shooting and none of them were injured.

The survivors were afraid that Amy Bishop left a so-called herpes bomb in one of the classrooms on her floor because she had access to the virus. Her research did include this particular strain and she has a vast knowledge on the topic so it was a possibility. The police would end up combing each and every floor in order to make sure nobody gets hurt once they open up the building again. No such device was found on the university grounds.

Her husband was informed of the events and he seemed to be shocked. It looked like he was completely in the dark about Amy's plans to get revenge over the tenure. The police questioned him back at the station and in his interview he stated that Amy called him after the shooting, pleading that he comes to the university in order to pick her up. Apparently, he refused to do it but certainly looks like she was waiting for him in front of the building.

Interrogation and psychological problems

When the police officers who were in charge of the investigation started talking to Bishop, it was clear that the woman was slightly delusional. She would constantly repeat sentences such as: "I wasn't there. It wasn't me." The interrogation was almost impossible due to Bishop's reluctant answers but she did acknowledge what she had done at the University of Alabama in Huntsville.

When we take a closer look at Bishop's past, it is evident that there were a lot of underlying psychological problems that went untreated. Her colleagues often described her as odd and quirky but she could also be very defensive and confrontational. After the attack at the restaurant and the probation sentence, her aggression became pretty well known. Those suggested anger management classes probably could have helped her a bit but they wouldn't solve everything.

The fact that she very likely murdered her brother back in the 1980s after a family quarrel and that Bishop continued living her life as if nothing happened could be interpreted as a narcissistic behavior combined with sociopathy. She had a hard time accepting the defeat and would often resolve the problems by acting aggressively towards the person she thought was responsible for her downfall which can be seen in the way she treated her supervisor at the Children's Hospital.

The law enforcement investigated this case furthermore and searched Bishop's house in order to find any evidence to what led to the shooting at the university. They took away her personal computer, as well as any documentation related to her firing from the teaching position. Amy Bishop was charged with one count of capital murder. Three charges of attempted murder were also included. Bishop decided not to involve the family attorney in her case and choose a court-appointed lawyer. The sentencing would either be life in prison or death penalty. There was a possibility for a parole in case she ends up in a prison.

Roy W. Miller who was her lawyer visited Bishop in the prison and did his own psychological evaluation before the two of them went to the court. Miller later said to the media that Bishop has serious mental problems and that she is probably bordering on paranoid schizophrenia. He even went very far and called his client „a wacko".

Miller would quickly retract his statements and say that Bishop's mind wasn't fully there during the shooting but he does understand that his client is undoubtedly guilty of the crime. His exact statement was: "This is not a whodunit. This lady has committed this offense or offenses in front of the world. It gets to be a question in my mind of her mental capacity at the time or her mental state at the time that these acts were committed."

Sentencing

Amy Bishop was the first professor or a faculty member in the history of the US who opened fire at a school or a university and murdered their own colleagues. She was clearly guilty because numerous survivors witnessed the entire event first hand and they were absolutely sure that Amy Bishop was the cold-blooded murderer.

In the meantime, the police re-investigated the case involving the murder of Bishop's brother back in 1986. After they took a closer look at the collected the physical evidence and files which were presumably lost, Amy Bishop was indicted. They determined she killed her brother as well and that it wasn't an accident as it was claimed by her mother.

This didn't help with Bishop's mental state at all and the problems piled up. Her attorney did say that Amy was feeling very sorry for the shooting at the University of Alabama in Huntsville a couple of weeks earlier. On 18th of June, 2010 Bishop tried to commit suicide while incarcerated but was rescued by the guards. After a short stint at the hospital, Bishop was transferred back to her jail cell but the guards kept a close eye on her and her behavior.

The preliminary trial began in September of 2011 but the final sentencing would arrive one year later. Amy Bishop stood in front of a crowded courtroom and pleaded not guilty. Roy W. Miller decided to use the insanity defense after sending his own psychiatrist to examine Bishop in the prison.

On 24th of September 2012, Amy Bishop was sentenced to life in prison. She wouldn't be able to appeal the verdict. She was also found guilty in Massachusetts for killing her brother but she wouldn't go to trial for that. Bishop did insist that she wanted to tell her story in front of the judges but Massachusetts refused to allow it because Alabama did have more strict punishments and the people in charge thought that life in prison is quite enough.

Amy Bishop didn't want to give up her possibility of an appeal so she tried to make a judge grant her a new opportunity. She filed a complaint in 2013 saying that her verdict wasn't explained to her properly and that she didn't understand the consequences. Two months later, she got an answer from the judge and her possibility of appeal was rejected. It is clear that Amy Bishop will spend the rest of her life behind the bars.

She is currently serving her time at Julia Tutwiler Prison for Women which is located in Wetumpka, Alabama. She continued to be a burden and Bishop's behavior didn't improve at all. She was involved in a physical attack on Amy Maclin who is a fellow inmate, injuring the woman. Bishop suffered a couple of bruises herself after Maclin used a tray in order to defend herself from her attacker.

This only proves that Bishop has anger management issues and that the insanity plea was purely for show. Bishop if fully aware of her actions and many experts who were closely following this case are certain that she planned the shooting at the University of Alabama in Huntsville for at least a couple of weeks before the crime.

LETHAL LOVERS: THE TRUE STORY OF CATHERINE MAY WOOD

JESSI DIXON

Lethal lovers

"You're going to hear about love. You are going to hear about jealously. You are going to hear about hatred," lawyer James Piazza told the jury during Gwendolyn Graham's trial in November 1989. "You will hear, through the testimony, about revenge. All (can be found) in heterosexual relationships. The same emotions are going to play here before you in the next week."

During the course of the trial, the jury listened to the story of Graham and Catherine May Wood – young lesbian lovers who enhanced their sexual play by killing elderly patients at the nursing home where they worked. Together, the two women would smother their victims, and on more than one occasion, would make love while washing the bodies of their recently murdered patients.

Wood and Graham met shortly after Graham moved from Texas to Michigan, where she took a job working with Wood at the Alpine Manor. The two women became fast friends, then lovers, by 1986 - and only two years later, they had been charged with the murders of five elderly patients.

Marguerite Chambers, age 60; Myrtle Luce, age 95; Mae Mason, age 79; Belle Burkhard, age 74; and Edith Cook, age 97, all lost their lives at the hands of these lethal lovers.

Pain and pleasure

After the marriage she'd entered into as a teenager broke up after seven years, Wood took a job at Alpine Manor in July 1985 – and was quickly promoted to supervisor of nurses aides. Despite her success on the job, Wood was still having trouble making friends, and at 450 pounds, she felt self-conscious about her appearance.

However, once Graham started working at Alpine Manor directly under Wood, her social life began to pick up. Together, the women began visiting gay bars, going to parties, and enjoying rough casual sex. Wood even started dieting.

According to Wood, Graham had initially brought up premeditated murder in October 1986, but she thought it was just part of a sexual game. By January 1987, Graham's desires had become more specific, and she told Wood she was interested in killing a patient.

"We were at home in the bedroom and she said she wanted to kill somebody at the Manor, and I just – that was about it, I didn't pay much attention," Wood confessed at Graham's trial.

"I asked her how, and she said she wanted to do it – she was going to suffocate them, and I said something about, with a pillow, and she said no she – that they would turn their heads, so that she would use washcloths to hole their nose and then their mouth. And I had asked her why, and she says to keep – because she would have to apply so much pressure that they would have indentations or bruises from pushing."

Wood claimed that Graham was a very dominant lover – often tying her down during sex and choking her or smothering her with a pillow until she nearly passed out. Wood never complained about Graham's aggressive lovemaking, and she started to recognize the similarities between pain and pleasure.

"Just talking about murder got them both excited," said a TruTV report about the killings. "The linked pain and pleasure of their sexual games became threaded with the idea of cruelty."

In an article published in the Williamson Daily News on December 7, 1988, Police Chief Walt Sprenger admitted that the intimate relationship between the two women was "part of a complex web that brings the whole thing together."

Too far gone

Wood received reduced charges thanks to a plea bargain agreement - spilling to the police all the details of the murders and testifying against Graham in her trial. Although Wood portrayed Graham as the criminal mastermind, her claims were refuted in a book by award-winning journalist Lowell Cauffiel, *Forever and Five Days*.

Released in 1992, the book explores the murders and the "love bond" shared by the two women.

Wood's account describes the first murder as taking place in January of 1987, when Graham smothered a patient suffering from Alzheimer's disease with a washcloth while Wood acted as a lookout. Too ill to defend herself, the woman became the couple's first victim - and since the death appeared to be of natural causes, there was no need for an autopsy. According to Wood, Graham claimed to have murdered the patient to "relieve her tension."

This first murder did help solidify the bond between Wood and Graham, as each felt confident that sharing the secret of the murder meant the other woman wouldn't be able to leave the relationship. "We were supposed to take turns killing so we could never leave each other," Wood stated in her testimony at Graham's trial.

The couple also enjoyed their success together – Graham had attempted to murder at least two targets who had been able to defend themselves before finally selecting a victim too far gone to fight back. They began selecting victims by pinching their noses to see if they would struggle.

"She was always real happy afterwards and I wanted her to be happy," Wood said. "I never told her 'no.' ... I never loved anybody the way I loved her."

As the next few months passed, Wood claimed Graham killed another four patients at Alpine Manor - who all ranged in age from 65 to 97. The women all suffered from Alzheimer's disease and were, according to Wood, incapacitated. In her testimony, Wood alleged that she and Graham started a game to select their next victim - trying to choose initials to spell out M-U-R-D-E. That became too difficult, and the women started counting each kill as a "day," referring to the phrase "I will love you forever and a day." Also introduced at the trial was a poem Wood wrote for Graham, which ended with, "you'll be mine forever and five days."

"Sometimes, the sheer excitement of the killing was too much," described one account of the events, "and they retired immediately to an empty room for sex while memories were fresh."

On other occasions, the couple would relive the murders after the fact – using the mementos Wood claimed that Graham had taken from each victim. However, these souvenirs were never found by the police, despite the fact that some accounts show that at least three nurses claimed they saw the shelf of souvenirs at the home Graham and Wood shared. These reportedly included an anklet, handkerchief, brooch, or a set of dentures.

Graham was also presented as being dominant in her relationship with Wood - sexually, physically, and emotionally, according to Wood's testimony. Graham reportedly even encouraged Wood to take on a more active role in their game – and asked her to kill a victim of her own to prove her love. Since she was unable to go through with it, she was transferred to another shift.

"I didn't think it was right," Wood said. "A lot of those people had a lot of life left in them and we were there to care for them, not abuse them."

Eventually, the relationship came to an end when Graham started seeing Heather Barager, another female nursing aide who worked with them at Alpine Manor, and the pair moved to Texas. Graham started working at a hospital, caring for infants. Wood and Graham still kept in touch via telephone.

According to Wood, Graham's new position working with infants encouraged her to come clean about the couple's murderous past.

"When she was killing people at Alpine and I didn't do anything, that was bad enough," Wood told the court at Graham's trial. "But when she would call me and say how she wanted to smash a baby, I had to stop her somehow. I knew she was working in a hospital there. She said she wanted to take one of the babies and smash it up against a window. I had to do something. I didn't care about myself anymore."

And so, Wood told her ex-husband, Ken Wood, about the murders she'd been involved with.

"It was nothing."

Wood was born on an army base in Washington state in March, 1962. Upon his return from Vietnam, Wood's father suffered from PTSD and frequent night terrors – and would often become emotionally and mentally abusive toward his two young daughers. According to Wood's sister Barbara Burns, the girls became quite close as a result of growing up in a "dysfunctional family."

"Cathy was a bookworm, she was very smart," Burns said. "She would stay in her bedroom and read. I think she also did that because she was tall and heavy, and the other kids could be very cruel to her, because of her size."

Her father was particularly cruel, Wood said, noting that he made her "feel real ugly" when she was around 12 or 13 – just as she began noticing a growing attraction to boys. However, Wood's first sexual experience ended up being with a woman.

"David" dressed as a man, and according to Wood, used a strap-on dildo during their sexual interactions. At first, Wood claims she didn't even know he was a woman.

One day, Wood placed a phone call to her friend Terry, which was received by his older brother Ken. She and Ken wound up chatting on the phone for five hours before she agreed to go out on a date with him – and, because of her experience with David, Wood slept with him on their first date just to be sure that he was actually a man.

However, Wood found their relationship unsatisfying – particularly sexually.

"I didn't like him touching me and I didn't like spending any time with him," Wood said. "Sex was just... it was nothing. Something you had to do, something you did because your husband wanted to. It wasn't fun, it wasn't interesting. He just did it and then went and watched football."

The couple married when Wood was only sixteen years old and pregnant. By all accounts, Wood was miserable in her marriage – she was depressed, overweight, neglected her housekeeping, and displayed little affection toward her daughter. Her relationship with Ken suffered, and the couple separated briefly in 1984 before attempting a reconciliation with the help of a marriage counselor.

As a teenager, Wood had worked as a candy striper at the hospital – and when she needed to find a job after finally leaving her husband in 1985, she decided to look into an open position at a nursing home called Alpine Manor to use some of the skills she'd developed. Shortly after she started working at the home, Wood said a coworker named Dawn started showing her attention – and, after her past experience with David, she started to question her sexuality.

But only three weeks into her new lesbian relationship with Dawn, Wood started spending more time with Graham – and only three weeks after that, the two moved in together. Initially, according to Wood, they were just going to be roommates, but she said that arrangement lasted "maybe five minutes" before they became lovers.

Wood said the relationship was satisfying, though, because she and Graham were "equals." They were a team who made decisions together – and with Graham, she said she learned that sex could be "nice."

"When Cathy met Gwen, it was the first time in her life that she ever sowed her oats," Burns said. "She'd been a stay-at-home person growing up, and when she got married to Ken, she never left the house. So when she separated from Ken and met Gwen, she started going out to movies, playing pool, started living for the first time in her life. But over time, she changed – she became hard."

A criminal mastermind

Still, Wood's confession to Ken about the murders wasn't the first time she had told her ex-husband something grisly – she'd confided in him years ago that she'd always been curious about what it would feel like to stab another person. Ken stalled for fourteen months before finally telling the police.

"I thought about the families of the victims; so many people were going to get hurt," said Ken, adding that he had promised his ex-wife that he wouldn't tell anyone. "But Cathy wasn't getting any better. I sensed a lot of guilt. She couldn't let go of what had happened ... I went to the police because she needed help."

An investigation began shortly, with Wood questioned extensively by the Walker Police Department's detectives. Slowly, she began to describe her version of the killings, pinning the majority of the blame on Graham.

"She would give tidbits, small information that led me to believe that she might possibly be involved in the actual killings," said Lieutenant Tom Freeman with the Walker Police Department. "At the same time, as an investigator, I had nothing to go on – only her testimony."

Two of the couple's victims were exhumed, as they had not been cremated, but a medical examination still revealed no physical evidence of foul play. According to Dr. Stephen Cohle, who examined the bodies of victims Marguerite Chambers and Edith Cook, cause of death could not be established based on the examination alone.

"There was no pathological evidence of suffocation," Cohle reportedly told the court. "However, there also was no overwhelming pathological evidence that natural conditions had caused their deaths."

Chambers' death certificate indicated that she died of a heart attack, which Cohle ruled out on his examination. While Chambers did have Alzheimer's disease, he stated she "could have lived perhaps several months, or possibly years longer." Cook's examination revealed narrowing in her coronary arteries, but Cohle noted that this was not severe enough to have been life-threatening.

"It's not that she couldn't have died of it, but it isn't very likely," he said. "(Police) don't go around looking for homicides where there is no evidence of homicide. I basically felt that the statements (made by Wood) were valid."

Since inconclusive results like this are consistent with many smothering cases, the deaths were still ruled as homicides by the medical examiner based on the information Wood had revealed to police. After warrants were issues for Wood and Graham's arrests, the women were brought in and charged with two murders in December of 1988.

"It is a case in which practically no physical evidence exists to prove a crime was committed," read an article published in the September 11, 1989 edition of the Argus-Press. "It appears to be based almost entirely on confessions from Graham's alleged accomplice and former lover, Catherine Wood."

During the trial, Wood continued to portray Graham as the criminal mastermind, claiming that Graham planned and committed each murder while Wood simply acted as a lookout. She was able to successfully plea-bargain down to a reduced sentence, and continued to maintain her innocence. Although there was no evidence to support Wood's allegations, Graham's new girlfriend did testify that Graham had confessed that she'd killed five patients - and the jury was convinced.

"Without you, I'm sure this matter never would have been cleared up," said Circuit Judge Robert Benson to Wood.

Graham received five life sentences from the court in November 1989, after she was found guilty of five counts of murder and one count of conspiracy to commit murder. She is currently serving her time in the Women's Huron Valley Correctional Facility in Michigan.

As for Wood, she received 20 years each on one count of second-degree murder and one count of conspiracy to commit second-degree murder. While she has been eligible for parole since March of 2005, Wood remains incarcerated in Federal Correctional Institution, a minimum security facility in Florida. Wood has been denied parole seven times, but her release is currently scheduled for June 6, 2021.

A "coercive and seductive pathological liar"

"There are two Cathy Woods, really. One of them wears a mask of sanity, and that mask portrays a relatively quiet, intelligent, articulate individual who seems at first, rather likeable and rather passive – not very aggressive at all," said Lowell Cauffiel. "But behind that mask is a cunning, manipulative psychopath."

Lowell Cauffiel's book, *Forever and Five Days*, depicts a dramatically different scenario. The non-fiction narrative explains how friends, family members, and coworkers who knew Wood and Graham said Wood was a "coercive and seductive pathological liar who delighted in wreaking havoc in the lives of others."

Tony Kubiak, who worked at Alpine Manor with both Wood and Graham, said that when he found out the facility was under investigation and that the police had identified two potential suspects, he surmised it may have something to do with Wood and someone else – possibly Graham.

"She's evil enough to kill," he said. "It wasn't (Graham) and somebody – it was (Wood) and somebody."

While Kubiak admitted Graham was likely the more violent of the two, Wood was the dominant one. Twice as big as Graham, and he had seen her pull Graham into a bedroom by her hair. He recalled Wood setting up pranks and revenge schemes while working at the home – she'd even threatened that he was on her "revenge list."

"She's insane," he said. "Cathy Wood is sick in the head."

In his book, Cauffiel offers compelling evidence to support a theory that Wood, in fact, planned that first murder as a way to guarantee Graham would never leave her - insurance she felt she needed after catching her lover with another woman.

"She tied me up to the bed, and she put a gun in between my legs ... and I was begging, because I thought she was going to shoot me,"

Graham said. "She just stood there for a minute, with it in me, and then she took it out and looked at me real strange, and then she left the house."

When even the secret of the murders wasn't enough to keep Graham from leaving her, Wood took the story to police - putting herself in legal jeopardy in order to seek revenge against her ex-lover. *Forever and Five Days* reveals a darker, more psychotic side to Wood, portraying her as the criminal mastermind who not only manipulated Graham into executing a series of murders but also manipulated the court to buy into her fabricated account.

According to Cauffiel's book, psychological testing done on Graham helped support the theory - as a sufferer of borderline personality disorder, Graham would be easy to manipulate. She also couldn't have been able to plan the sophisticated series of murders, or effectively defend herself during the trial.

"Gwen Graham is very mixed-up woman who comes out of a childhood involving a certain amount of abuse. (She's) a very dependent individual, a person eager to please the partner that she's with – somewhat of a tragic figure, actually," Cauffiel said.

The size difference between the two women also stuck with several witnesses and audience members of the trials. The granddaughter of Mae Mason, one of the couple's victims, watched as Wood sobbed through her questioning during the trial.

"It just astounded me that a three-hundred-pound woman could feel so afraid of Gwen Graham," said eighteen-year-old Stephanie Engman. "She was *too* sorry for what she had done."

Inmates who were incarcerated with Wood also reveal in the book that she told them two versions of the story that did not support the version she told police. In the first, she claimed to have invented the entire story to punish Graham for leaving her, and in the second, she confessed that she'd committed all the murders - but, to exact her revenge, she'd framed Graham for it.

"Yeah, I did it," inmate Margaret Mann remembered Wood saying. "Gwen was the lookout. Gwen watched my back."

In her testimony, Graham fervently denied the accusations that she had smothered patients – and even claimed that she didn't know of any murders that had even occurred at the home. In fact, Graham alleged that Wood frequently concocted rumors that she would spread around the nursing home, and Graham only went along with them to humor Wood.

"I was not present at the time of any of these people's deaths," Graham said. "I was somewhere in the building, working. That's all I know."

The murder plot, she said, was one Wood's "head games," just a joke. Until Graham started seeing another woman, and Wood began threatening to take the story to the police. Eventually, when she realized the police had been investigating the deaths, Graham concluded that Wood "was going to get even, just like she said she was."

"She wanted to know If it was true, and if it was true, she wasn't going to take the whole blame for (the slayings)," said Baragar in her testimony at Graham's trial. "Cathy was a part of it."

Graham also refuted the testimonies of some of her friends and former lovers, who claimed that Graham had confessed to smothering patients – but Graham said she'd only been relating to them the fabricated story Wood had come up with. According to an article from the September 19, 1989 edition of the Argus-Press, Graham was "visibly shaken" as Baragar recounted her "confessions."

Her decision to leave Wood and move to Texas with Barager, Graham said, was because she'd gotten "tired of playing games, hurting people ... The games just got out of hand."

Her lawyer, James Piazza, did make a request that the charges against Graham be reduced or dismissed entirely, due to a lack of evidence. When the motion was denied by Judge Roman Snow, Piazza closed his argument by saying that the murder spree was entirely concocted by a vindictive Wood, who was looking to get even with her ex-lover by any means necessary.

"Gwen Graham is living in a horror right now because of the bizarre imagination of Cathy Wood," he said. "Just because (Wood) pleaded guilty doesn't mean Gwen Graham is guilty of anything – other than going along with bad jokes."

However, the jury accepted Wood's account of the events. According to jury foreman Glenn Russell, "we felt it was a story that nobody could just think up."

"Sometimes, I would like to say I just made it up," Wood said. "That would be so easy. And then everybody could just go back to being happy again, I guess. But that's not so."

Facing the fallout

"I had always been pleased with Alpine," said Linda Engman, daughter of victim Mae Mason. "I remember that phone call from the nursing home like it was yesterday. I was flabbergasted."

Alpine Manor was faced with lawsuits from several of the families of the victims, claiming they had hired "dangerous and unbalanced employees." According to a spokeswoman for the nursing home, Ginny Seyferth, counseling was provided to employees following the arrests – as police began investigating eight "suspicious" deaths that occurred between January to April 1987.

"Alpine Manor is devastated, but relieved that something is being done," Seyferth told news reporters in December 1988. "Both had very good reviews. Both were well-liked by the patients."

Alpine Manor has since shut down. The building is now home to a new nursing home, Sanctuary at Saint Mary's.

Ken is still struggling to come to terms with his ex-wife's actions – and the burden that places on their daughter.

"Am I going to be able to give my child a normal upbringing, with her knowing who her mother is?" Ken said. "She can't hide that fact. That's what angers me."

Wood, who remains incarcerated, attempted to illegally solicit a penpal in 2013 by posting an ad on an online dating site. While inmates in Florida are welcome to receive mail from pen pals, they are strictly prohibited from seeking them out.

"Teach me! I've been incarcerated for two decades," Wood's profile stated. "I go to the parole board soon and I need someone who's kind and patient to teach me about the exciting new things in the world. I'm looking for a friend, male or female, to teach me everything I forgot. Are you honest? I am honest and non-judgmental. We can talk about anything and everything. I've never done drugs and I don't smoke. I like to play and have fun. Do you have time for a good friend?"

Graham, on the other hand, still maintains her innocence – claiming even years later that the entire story was fabricated by Wood to punish her for leaving.

"I'm innocent," Graham said. "I can no more prove that I'm innocent than they ever proved that I was guilty. I'm stuck here because of her word."

According to Ken Kolker with the Grand Rapids Press, we may never know what really happened with the Alpine Manor murders.

"When you look into different cases, you almost always get this gut feeling that either they did it or they didn't do it," he said. "And this is one of those cases where you gut feeling is that I don't know if it even happened – and if it happened, I don't know who was running the show."